Changing the Process
of
Teaching & Learning

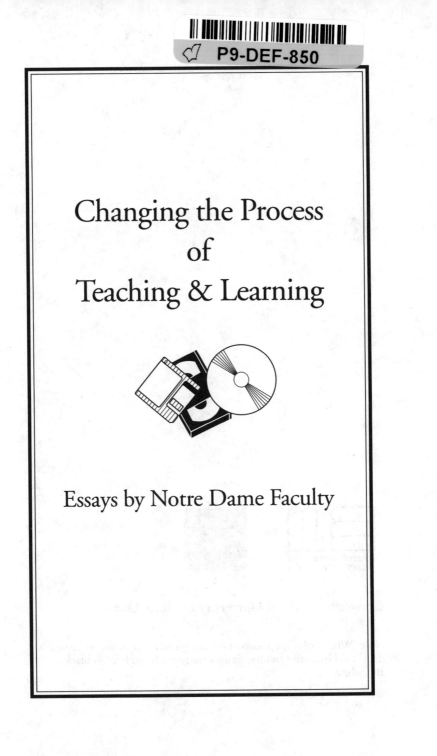

Essays by Notre Dame Faculty

Educational Media
University of Notre Dame

Copyright © 1994, University of Notre Dame

Note: While color is an important design element in the materials developed by many faculty, figures are reproduced here in black and white.

Table of Contents

This book contains only a few of the Notre Dame faculty and student success stories from 1992 to 1994: success in the use of advanced educational technologies; success in redoubling of enthusiasm; success in improved classroom interactivity; success in reaching beyond the classroom to open new highways of communication; success in multimedia courseware development; success in preparing students to achieve in groups and teams as well as individually. We wish to thank the faculty, staff, and students who have helped bring about such rapid, coherent change.

Finally, this book was shepherded to press by Michael Langthorne of Educational Media. Compilation, editing, layout, and cover design was by C. Joseph Williams of the Office of University Computing.

It was in 1978 when I first became Provost that Sister Elaine DesRosiers came to talk with me about her dream of an ideal Educational Media Center at Notre Dame. At that time both of us believed that the reality was somewhere on the distant horizon! But Elaine is a persistent dreamer.

The generous gift from the DeBartolo family for a new classroom building presented a perfect opportunity. In cooperation with the Office of University Computing, Elaine and her dedicated staff began the planning process to provide the best in technological support for teaching a new generation of students who grew up with technology.

With the opening of DeBartolo in Fall, 1992 and a series of well-developed workshops to introduce faculty to these new tools, a virtual revolution took place on this campus. And each year more faculty join those demanding classroom space and technical support in DeBartolo's remarkable facilities.

This book bears effective witness to the variety of creative ways Notre Dame faculty has put this technology to use.

In my own field of mathematics, experimentation in mathematics education occurs, of course, in the obvious use of computers and visual displays in areas involving numerical analysis. But computerization also has great potential in symbolic manipulation, in the shaping of geometrical forms, in dynamic illustrations of infinite limiting processes, and more.

Each of you can discover similar ways of transforming the materials of your field into visual effects which make teaching and learning a whole new experience.

The dream has come true.

I am very pleased to see its prompt incorporation into the academic life of this campus.

My special thanks to the DeBartolo family, to Elaine and her staff, to the Office of Universty Computing, and to all of you for your imaginative responses to this opportunity which gives us and our students a head start into the 21st Century!

Timothy O'Meara
Provost

A climate of change and redefinition has surrounded higher education in recent years. Financial pressures, changes in students, continuing growth in research output are all forcing a rethinking of the nature of the academic enterprise. For better or worse, or probably both, technology is an element in these matters. Indeed, the University of Notre Dame recently made a large investment in enhancing the technological infrastructure of the campus. Much has had to do with the classroom.

Since the the opening of DeBartolo Hall, use of the Media-On-Call system, computer presentation, and the merger of the two has increased the understanding of ways technology can influence the effectiveness of classroom presentations. More than half of the faculty have used Media-On-Call for basic classroom media presentation; more than 10% have been awarded JumpStart grants to develop and use computer and multimedia programs in the classroom. Some of the teachers in DeBartolo Hall classrooms have made use of much broader applications available to them; for example, they can bring into the classroom information from their office computer, or from elsewhere on campus, or from almost anywhere in the world through the network connection in the classroom. In the rooms that have computers at every workplace, members of the class work together and critique one another's work. In some cases, the instructor has acted as a group mentor.

A natural question for each member of the faculty is, "How might these technological factors change activities in which I am involved?" The articles in this book reflect the answers to that question given from a variety of perspectives by professors who have assumed the challenge of using the technology. The common theme is that modern technology has significant potential to enhance the teaching/learning environment.

Elaine V. DesRosiers, O.P , Ed.D.
Director of Educational Media

Donald Z. Spicer, Ph.D.
Assistant Provost
Office of University Computing

Charles R. Crowell
Paul D. Worland
Department of Psychology

Behavioral Instruction and Computers:
An 18 Year Experience at Notre Dame

Introduction

Precipitated by the completion of DeBartolo Hall in 1992,
and as evidenced by the present compilation of articles, the
University of Notre Dame is presently witnessing a burgeon-
ing of the use of computer technologies in the classroom
environment. While DeBartolo Hall can be seen as the
catalyst for the development and application of such technologies, the successful utilization of computers in the
classroom has a long tradition within the University. This
tradition goes back at least as far as Bill Davisson's pioneering
work with computer-assisted instruction in economics (see
Davisson & Bonello, 1976). Also, within the Department of
Psychology, the integration of computers into the structure
of the classroom experience occurred as early as 16 B.D.
(Before DeBartolo). The result of these efforts is Psychology
211A, otherwise known to past and present students as
Personalized System of Instruction (PSI).

General Properties of the PSI Method

The PSI method of instruction was first developed at the
University of Brasilia by a group of four psychologists

1

charged with the task of creating a Department of Psychology at the University of Brasilia. Spurred by a general dissatisfaction with the traditional college lecture format, these psychologists, among them Fred Keller, developed a learning procedure based upon known principles of learning and reinforcement theory. The resultant teaching methodology became known as the "Keller Plan" and later was renamed to the PSI method (see Sherman & Ruskin, 1978). Five distinctive features characterize the Personalized System of Instruction.

Self-Paced Progress. Within certain constraints, students are permitted to progress through the course at a speed that best suits their individual abilities, learning styles, and other time demands.

Small Units of Material. The material to be learned is divided into small, manageable units. Students progress one unit at a time, rather than dealing with large blocks of information as is often done in traditional college courses.

Unit Mastery. A unit mastery requirement demands that students attain a specified mastery criterion before moving on to the next unit. If students fail to attain the mastery requirement on the first attempt of a unit exam, they are simply encouraged to re-study those parts of the unit that were not mastered and retake an alternate form of the unit exam, without penalty.

Written Material. Information to be learned in the course is contained entirely in textbook(s), written study guides and written unit learning objectives. Thus, all course material is constantly accessible to students. This feature means that lectures and/or demonstrations are used as motivational tools or as rewards for completing a predetermined amount of material by a particular date, rather than as sources of critical information.

Student Proctors. Student proctors (who have previously mastered the course content) are an integral part of the course. The original role of the proctors was to administer and score unit exams, to remediate students when they fail to master a unit, and to serve as general resource people who can clarify material and answer any questions students might have about the course material.

PSI at Notre Dame

Beginning in 1976, the PSI method as outlined above was instituted at Notre Dame for one section of Introductory Psychology. Several difficulties of implementing this method quickly became apparent. One of these difficulties centers on the fact that all tests consisted of short answer/oral questions and thereby had to be individually scored by a proctor. The amount of administrative work that these tasks entail necessitated a large proctor force (8-10 student proctors) to ensure the smooth operation of courses the size of typical Introductory Psychology classes. A second drawback was student procrastination. The flexibility of a self-paced format allows students the freedom to finish early, and also to start late. A third and final obstacle involved the mastery requirement. Because students are typically required to be perfect, or near perfect, in their performance on unit tests means that a sufficient number of alternate test forms must be created to accommodate the highest possible number of retakes. Moreover, the mastery criterion also implies that if students finish all required units, their performance will be "perfect" by definition. Hence anyone, and everyone, can get an "A." This feature can tend to provoke discomfort in administrative circles.

Computerization of PSI

In an attempt to address some of these implementation pitfalls, we focused our efforts on the development of an interactive computer system. It seemed that a computer could assume many of the routine administrative chores normally performed by student proctors, including test administration and record keeping. Such an interactive system would free the proctors to devote more of their energies toward answering questions and being a resource to students than would otherwise be possible. This would also

3

serve to reduce the need for a large proctor staff. In addition, computerized test scoring almost certainly would require a move away from short answer/oral tests to more objective test formats, greatly simplifying problems of objectivity and consistency associated with grading written or oral tests.

The culmination of these efforts was a software course management system called PROCTOR which has been used in our PSI course since spring semester of 1979. The PROCTOR system has evolved from a PL/1 based version for the IBM 370/168 mainframe computer operating in a timesharing environment (see Crowell, Quintanar, and Grant, 1981), to a version programmed in Applesoft BASIC and run on a network of Apple II microcomputers, to the current version programmed in RBASE and run on networked IBM compatible microcomputers. This PROCTOR system allows students to logon to the system using a personal class ID, access a course newsletter, take tests, receive performance feedback on individual test items as well as the completed test, and monitor their own progress through the course. The system is available to students only during 2-hour sessions 3 times a week (the regularly scheduled class time). This computerized approach to PSI allows the instructor and student proctor to create, modify, or display test questions and answers, course parameters, the course newsletter, and any aspects of a student's record.

Many of the difficulties associated with the manual implementation of the PSI method are indeed remedied by the interactive PROCTOR system. Student proctors are freed from having to attend continuously to administrative details, thus reducing the number of student proctors needed to as few as two per class period. Tests are delivered and scored on-line, performance data are stored and student records are updated immediately. Automating these duties assures up-to-the minute completeness and accuracy of student records, making it easier to keep track of both individual and class progress. PROCTOR also helps curb the procrastination often observed in PSI courses by administering a bonus point system for timely course unit completion. Such bonus point systems have been effectively utilized by others for this

4

purpose, but only at the expense of creating further administrative duties for the proctors. The present bonus point system is completely computer controlled thereby eliminating such drawbacks.

PSI Enrollment at Notre Dame

As illustrated by Figure 1, approximately 2300 students have been enrolled in the Introductory Psychology PSI course over the past 36 semesters. These figures do not include a significant number of students who have enrolled in the PSI course for the summer semesters of these academic years.

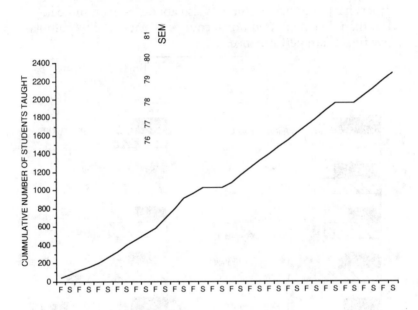

Figure 1. Cumulative number of students taught Introductory Psychology at Notre Dame with the PSI method (main graph) and the number of students taught each semester (inset).

Student Reactions to PSI

Through an examination of course evaluations, several important differences emerge between traditional-format sections of introductory psychology and the section employing the PSI format (see Figure 2). In general, as compared to students in the lecture section, students in the PSI section have rated the course as involving more work than other courses. Even so, (again as compared to students in a normal lecture section) PSI students also rated the course more positively on dimensions such as enjoyment of the course, amount learned, personal value of the course, clarity of learning objectives, specification of performance criteria, degree of motivation to learn, meaningfulness of final course grade, personal value of the course, and recommendation of the course to others. In addition, in tests we and others have conducted, students also appear to learn more in PSI than they do in traditional courses as evidenced by cumulative final exam performance.

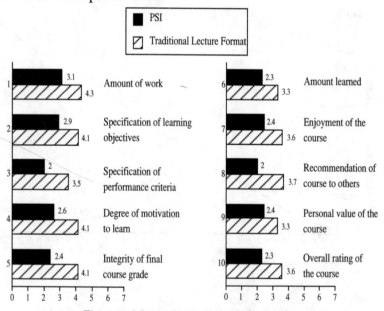

Figure 2. Mean ratings to 10 class evaluation items by students in a PSI or traditional lecture format Introductory Psychology course, where 1 = more/better than other courses at Notre Dame and 7 = less/worse than other courses at Notre Dame.

6

Implications for the Educational Environment

Our experience over the years with the PSI method, in both its traditional and computerized form, suggests that the use of instructional technology in the classroom may have some important implications for the general educational environment of the University that need to be considered, if not debated.

The Student's Role. The PSI method in particular, and other forms of instructional technology as well, affords the student a great deal of flexibility and responsibility in terms of the learning process. In contrast to traditional courses, students in a PSI course choose the pace with which they work through the material. They can spend as much or as little time on a particular unit as their schedules allow and their learning styles demand. Some students can (and do) finish the course material early. The underlying assumption here is that the burden of responsibility for many decisions about how and when learning will take place properly belongs with the learner, not with the instructor.

The Instructor's Role. Skinner long ago argued that, from a behavioral point of view, there are many circumstances under which the most appropriate role for a teacher is to be a manager of the educational environment instead of a personal purveyor of critical information (see Skinner, 1968). The PSI method, along with other forms of instructional technology, is clearly founded on that proposition. As a manager, an instructor or teacher becomes less concerned with personally delivering instruction and more concerned with facilitating the learning process by providing effective materials, support systems, and incentives for the learner.

The Concept of Academic Performance. The very idea of instructional technology as a way to engineer and deliver more effective instruction forces us to examine our most basic views about student performance and progress. Traditionally, educators here at Notre Dame and elsewhere have tended to assume such things as : (a) not all students in a class can (or should) get an "A;" (b) a course should involve someone standing up in front of the class giving lectures; (c) students must actually come to a physical place called a class in order to learn; and (d) the time-frame for learning is a semester, so courses should take that long to complete and finals must occur only at the end of the semester. Obviously, technological innovations like the PSI method, computer-based learning, and distance learning (to name only a few) violate one or more of these assumptions about student performance and progress.

Are we ready for the possible changes in our views and methods of education that instructional technologies may bring?

References

Crowell, C.R., Quintanar, L.R., & Grant, K. L. (1981). PROCTOR: An on-line student evaluation and monitoring system for use with PSI format courses. Behavior Research Methods & Instrumentation, 13(2), 121-127.

Davisson, W.I. & Bonello, F.J. (1976). Computer-Assisted Instruction in Economic Education. Notre Dame, Indiana: University of Notre Dame Press.

Sherman, J.G. & Ruskin, R.S. (1978). The Instructional Design Library. Englewood Cliffs, New Jersey: Educational Technology Publications.

Skinner, B.F. (1968). The Technology of Teaching. New York: Appleton-Century Crofts.

Lyn Spillman
Sociology Department

Using Email For Class Writing and Discussion

Introduction

Teaching an introductory sociology seminar of around 25 students, I try to provide the resources and the environment which will best promote students' own discovery and empowerment. I recently redesigned this class to incorporate and test the use of an electronic mail (email) class list as a device which might offer another channel of student reflection, discussion, and engagement with their own research. I was particularly keen to increase the amount of learning through dialogue which could take place, and to have students develop an ease with writing and with the more disciplined reflection which writing allows. Here, I assess the uses I made of email to promote class goals, students' responses to email assignments, and students' overall reaction to the use of email in class.

Implementation

While there are a variety of ways email might be used in classes, I aimed especially to use email for work eliciting shared reflection about the relevance of crucial concepts through shared written examples, for email summaries of original research projects and discussion of findings, and for exercises in comprehension of more challenging reading

9

assignments. I also encouraged more frequent personal communication as students developed research topics and designs.

Students could communicate to the class as a whole, using a class email address, and they could also send messages to me. In the second week of class our technical assistant, Uma Balakrishnan, explained to students how to get an email account, and how to use it. This introduction to email took about a class and a half. Uma was also available to help students with specific problems. Later in the semester, another half class was devoted to explaining how to create mailboxes to sort messages received.

Email writing was assigned every two weeks, and about half of the class also used email to explain ideas, doubts, and questions they had individually about their research projects. The design of the email assignments was unproblematic: they were simply developments of questions and discussions which are used in any seminar, and required little adaptation from earlier classes. I told students when I would be reading and responding to email messages. Because I was testing the use of email in this class, and expected unforeseen difficulties, I did not assign separate grades for the exercises but counted them towards the class participation portion of the grade..

The Uses of Email

(1) <u>Class Preparation</u> As I prepared classes, student responses in email exercises allowed me to assess where understanding was relatively weak and prepare accordingly. They also allowed me to develop examples and issues which students had raised. While these two contributions to class preparation could be made by other sorts of discussion and assignment, email eased and expanded my ability to prepare classes to address more closely student responses.

Exercises asking that students develop their own examples of concepts and arguments discussed in class were most helpful in contributing to my ability to prepare classes in this more dialogic way. These exercises were also popular with students: one student commented, "I liked using personal examples. It gives a chance for students to get to know more about you outside of class." However, two other students felt that the email assignments were "too impersonal:" "I would rather discuss [the email message topics] in class." (The email work was an addition, and not a replacement, of course, to class discussion.)

(2) <u>Generating Dialogue</u> The exercise which was most effective in generating dialogue and reflection, and most popular with students in their evaluations, was an assignment to write an abstract of their completed research findings. Their research projects were independently formulated within class guidelines, and topics differed widely. In responding to the abstracts, students commented thoughtfully on the implications of others' findings, and raised questions about research design on the basis of their own work to design research. Thinking about other peoples' topics seemed to generate very productive discussions about issues which concerned them, but also discussions which were mostly using what students had learnt in class to further that discussion. The majority of students who had a favorite email exercise chose this one, commenting, for example "I enjoyed the abstracts and reading about others' work and everyone's opinion of them" and "I liked responding to what other people had to say as opposed to just answering questions," and "I liked when we shared and discussed findings from our research papers. It was really interesting to hear about these."

In future I would incorporate assignments generating this sort of discussion earlier in the design of the research project. I would also require a response to one or two other responses in any exercise demanding personal reflection; while students enjoy the discussion, they did not initiate it, at least at the level of the class list.

(3) "<u>Normal Homework Exercises</u>" Exercises requiring straightforward answers to questions about the main arguments and evidence in some more challenging reading were least popular with students. A majority naming the least

appealing exercise named this one, commenting "I didn't find it very interesting," and "Who cares to read 25 summaries?" and "It was too much like a normal homework exercise."

But an exam question on that material generated very competent responses, much better than a similar question the previous time I taught the class, so I would still occasionally use email this way. I would, however, ask students to send their responses to me directly, rather than mail them to the class. The advantage over 'normal homework exercises' is that more specific and longer corrections and comments for each student are easier and quicker to generate.

(4) <u>Individual Discussion and Feedback</u> About half the class also wrote to me with questions and draft research designs in the course of the semester, and with a few students email messages became an ongoing conversation about their research as it developed. My impression is that these students were shyer in conversation than those who typically discuss their work at length, and that email was an encouragement to them. Pedagogically, the advantage of this written questioning and conversation was the more detailed understanding of their questions I could develop (and, I suspect, which they developed in the writing), and the more specific and detailed responses I could give. This email discussion took little time and was very productive. It did not, of course, replace other meetings and phonecalls. However, one student commented that "I would rather talk to professors personally."

Student Attitudes to Email Technology

The majority of students reported that their first response to the prospect of email work was negative, although a substantial minority were intrigued by the idea or already enjoyed email. But many later changed their attitude; most said their attitudes were later positive.

At first, surprisingly few had experience with email, and some were daunted by using it. They commented: "I was worried I wouldn't be able to work it," "I was annoyed because I have tried to understand it and have always failed—I didn't want to try again" and "I was scared because I have a history of horrible difficulties with computers."

Moreover, thirteen students dropped the class, many more than had done so previously; they were all women, and they all disappeared after the introduction to using email. While I have no evidence that they dropped because they were intimidated, like the persistent student above, by the use of email, one overwhelmed and annoyed woman did tell me early that she "enjoyed language... was a literature student... couldn't deal with all this." If it's possible that arts and letters students are often daunted by any use of a computer, then this would be a good reason for going slowly in introducing email assignments.

But many students who were daunted at first later changed their attitude. Some wrote with surprise and excitement: "it was easier to operate than I'd thought," "After it was set up, I realized how simple the system is" and "Email taught me not to fear computers. I even like them now."

The minority of students who disliked email at the end of the semester felt that "it was kind of a burden" or "it became a big hassle—I was unaware of the technicalities." Few actually reported practical difficulties in doing the assignments, however. Of those who did report practical difficulties, making the trip to the labs seemed the biggest problem. Although some worried, as I did, that actually getting a computer would be hard, this did not seem to prevent them doing the assignments on time, and I heard few explanations or complaints based on computer availability. However, in the future I would not assign exercises in the last week or two of class, because several students suggested that was the busiest time at the labs.

The majority of students reported the class introduction to email was helpful—"Uma really helped me," "Uma was a big help." However, in future I would make sure the introduction was held in a lab rather than a classroom, and students worked together as they learnt how to use email. Several colleagues have suggested that pairing more and less confident students would be useful.

Students appreciated very much the availability of someone assigned to this class to help with their technical problems, as indeed did I. I was struck by the warmth of the reliance on Uma's help—"My account is all messed up. Uma will fix it"—and I believe that, for some of these students at least, the personal attention available throughout the class was very important for the success of the email assignments. I believe that students would not have developed a positive attitude if I had only required them to go to an email class provided by the Office of University Computing. Until students develop familiarity with electronic mail, and come into classes with the account and the skills they need to use it, it seems important not to overestimate their preparation. While we are unlikely to have the luxury of a technical assistant in most of our classes, it seems important to pay a lot of attention to introducing students to help at Office of University Computing, and following up to diffuse practical frustrations they encounter.

Conclusions

Email worked as an additional tool for encouraging reflection on class materials and developing dialogue, between students and myself, and between students themselves. Most successful was the use of email discussion between students about their research projects, and I would plan such discussion earlier in a future class. Assignments demanding personal reflection on class materials were also a helpful addition for class preparation and for student engagement. Assignments which demanded similar replies or simple 'right or wrong' answers added least to the class.

For successful use of email in the future, I would ensure that (1) students are required to respond to the messages of others—they enjoy this but did not initiate it (2) that their introduction to email was held in the labs and that they worked in collaborative groups (3) for the time being, that no major weight of assessment was put on email assignments and that (4) practical fears and frustrations were diffused as much as possible, by making personal connections between students and people who can answer their questions.

Jay B. Brockman
Department of
Computer Science and Engineering

Use of DeBartolo Multimedia Facilities in Teaching Computer Science and Engineering Classes

The multimedia classrooms in DeBartolo Hall have had a profound impact on the way that Computer Science and Engineering classes have been taught at Notre Dame. While we have yet to experiment with self-paced, interactive "courseware"—as has been tried at some universities—we have found that the ability to project a computer screen in a classroom has many advantages over a chalkboard or transparencies in teaching computer courses in a standard lecture format. In this essay, we'd like to share our experiences in using the DeBartolo facilities in two of our courses: a sophomore-level introductory programming course and a junior-level computer hardware design course.

CSE 232 is a sophomore-level, introductory computer programming course. Presently, it is required of all Computer Science, Computer Engineering, and Electrical Engineering students. The course is also a prerequisite for all upper-level courses in the department, and hence has a significant enrollment of students from other majors such as Mathematics. While an important aspect of the course is to impart the basic skills of working with the "C" programming language and the Unix operating system, fundamentally the goal of the course is to teach students how to solve problems using a computer. Many topics in the course thus transcend the use of any particular programming language, and rather focus upon the basic abstractions used in representing problems and their solutions, and showing how these abstractions may then be mapped into a computer program.

In order to teach this material effectively, it is our philosophy that three topical threads must be spun and woven simultaneously throughout the course. The first thread is teaching problem solving strategy, which includes techniques such as how to simplify a problem by decomposing it. The second thread is showing how algorithmic solutions to problems may be expressed in a particular programming language, in this case "C." The third thread is training students in the proper use of programming tools such as editors, compilers, and debuggers. All to often, this last thread is either taught without regard to the other two or is left for the students to learn on their own. The consequence of this is analogous to a football player with basic blocking and tackling skills but no knowledge of strategy or game management, or conversely, an armchair quarterback. The challenge in teaching an introductory programming course is thus to find a way to effectively intertwine these three threads in a lecture.

The DeBartolo multimedia classrooms provide an excellent setting for doing just that. In particular, we have used the Sun workstation, running a window manager, to display several simultaneous views of a given lecture topic. The Sun workstations are also the computers that the students use for their programming assignments. Figure 1 below shows a typical screen that would be projected in the classroom. In this example, the screen consists of two windows: first, a desktop publishing package (FrameMaker) with the lecture notes, and second, a graphical software debugging package (xdbx) that displays a running "C" program. While the lecture notes provide an English description and an illustration of an algorithm for drawing a box with nested loops, the debugger allows us to step through the execution of the corresponding program, with the arrow indicating the current instruction. Lectures are thus animated in a manner that would be impossible with traditional classroom media.

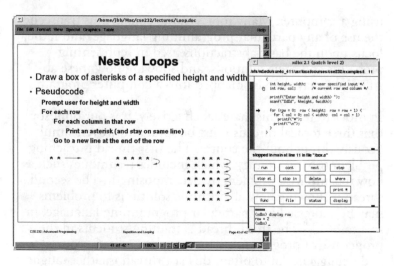

Figure 1. Example screen from sophomore-level computer programming class.

Our junior-level computer hardware design course has much in common with the sophomore-level programming course. As with the programming course, emphasis in the hardware design course is placed on problem solving and design principles: the major difference lies in the fact that solutions are implemented in hardware rather than software (or a combination of hardware and software). Students in this course use a commercial CAD package, running on the Sun workstations, that is produced by the Mentor Graphics Corporation. Tools in this package include a drafting tool for capturing a design, as well as simulators for analyzing the behavior and performance of a design. In much the same manner as with our programming class, we project multiple windows from the workstation in the classroom to highlight different points during a lecture. Figure 2 shows a screen from the hardware design course. One window contains the lecture notes describing a design problem, while another window shows a view of circuit that implements a solution to this problem.

18

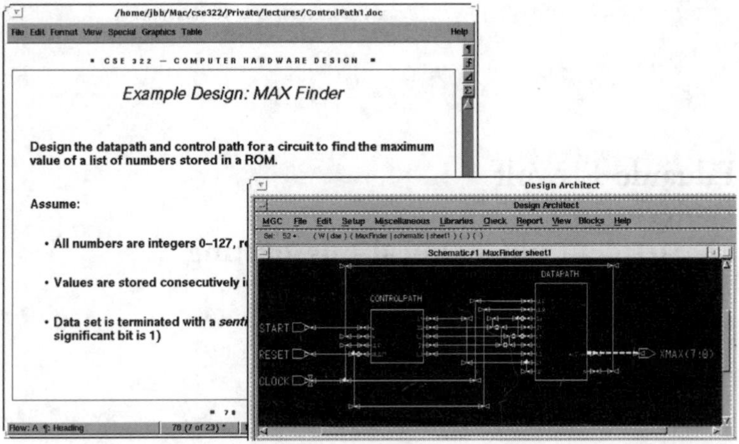

Figure 2. Example screen from junior-level computer hardware design class.

In summary, our conclusions should come as no surprise: the ability to project a computer image in the classroom is an invaluable asset for teaching Computer Science and Engineering classes. Not only does this provide the obvious advantages of demonstrating the programming environment to students, but using a computer in the classroom also opens the door to more flexible teaching methods.

Eduardo E. Wolf
Professor
Department of Chemical Engineering

Interactive Teaching With Computers

My style of teaching as a professor of Chemical Engineering is via interaction with the class. It is very difficult to reach everyone in a class of more than 20 students and get them involved in thinking about the subject. They frequently become spectators and do not learn from the class experience. A classroom equipped with computers connected to a network, however, provides an excellent opportunity to reach simultaneously all the students in the class. At the same time the students can get involved in the subject by having them develop the lessons rather than having the professor present them to the students.

Since no software was available to conduct this type of teaching, I developed my own. In this format (I called it Electronic Tutor) most of my lectures are presented as problems that the students solve during class. The program asks questions about a specific problem being analyzed. On that basis, the students develop the equations pertaining to the problem and solve them. The software has a special menu and fonts to facilitate typing the equations. In addition, there are regular lectures wherein the principles applicable to a class of problems are presented. These lectures can be copied onto a disk after class. At the beginning of the semester, students are given solutions to the lessons, later on, they have to submit the lessons along with their homework.

To make sure everyone is participating in this effort, the software has a feature that permits me to display in front of the class the computer screen of a selected student. The selection is made by clicking simulated dice which randomly selects a student from an available class list. The screen displayed, which reflects the selected student's work, is then used as a point of discussion so that the rest of the class can adjust their results to the correct answer. Thereafter, the students resume their work until the solution is reached. One of the interesting features of this type of interaction is that it allows me to evaluate the level of understanding reached at that point by the students. I also realize which are the major errors made and misconceptions acquired. It is especially very telling to see how much the students have forgotten the basic subjects, i.e. math, which is supposed to help them to solve the problems being analyzed.

So far the effort has paid off. The return from the first exam yielded a 15 point improvement in the average compared to last year. Above all, it has made my teaching more interesting and rewarding. If I cannot enjoy what I am teaching, I cannot expect the students to get interested in the subject either. Interactive teaching provides an opportunity to do that, and thus it improves educational technology. I am certain that in the future this trend will overtake classical lecture-based teaching. For this to happen it is necessary that more resources in both hardware and software become available. Right now, room 331 DeBartolo Hall, the only one equipped with Macintosh computers,is used mainly by the freshman writing program, and is only available at 8 am on Tuesdays and Thursdays! It is a real challenge to keep students awake at that time. When I use the interactive software, most students do not notice when the end of the class period is reached, which speaks for itself about the advantages of getting students involved in the learning process.

Patrick Sain
Department of Electrical Engineering

Computer Technology in Technical Education

The use of computer technology in education is increasing at a rate that not only taxes institutions' abilities to keep pace, but also challenges instructors and students. Nonetheless, despite the effort involved in keeping abreast of the state of the art, with its rapid hardware and software developments and upgrades, many are quick to agree that the benefits of such technology in education are substantial.

This article provides a brief overview of some of the uses of computer technology in the engineering and science curricula on campus. The categories considered are the use of computer technology in analysis, design, and simulation and its use in assisting and augmenting classroom instruction.

Analysis, Design, and Simulation

Software packages utilizing color graphics and high-resolution screens make analysis, design, and simulation among the more exciting areas of educational technology. Many of these packages are highly specialized and sophisticated programs that facilitate the design and simulation of complex systems in a particular technical field.

Mentor Graphics, for example, is a collection of software tools that facilitates virtually all stages of computer chip design, from logic simulation to the physical layout of the chip itself. Used in six different courses at all levels in the Computer Science and Engineering Department, and in one course in the Electrical Engineering Department, Mentor Graphics allows students to represent complex circuit designs as symbolic diagrams composed of interconnections of standard components selected from menus. Dr. Eugene Henry, Professor of Computer Science and Engineering and vice-president of the Mentor Graphics User's Group, points out that some student designs can involve a few thousand transistors—an accomplishment all but impossible by hand. Furthermore, said Henry, because Mentor Graphics is widely used in industry, companies are interested in hiring Notre Dame students because of their familiarity with the software.

Perhaps the most pervasive software in technical education is Matlab, a program that facilitates matrix algebra (Matlab stands for "matrix laboratory"). Matlab offers users a powerful and user-friendly programming syntax that tremendously simplifies the handling of mathematical equations involving matrices. Combined with powerful color graphics output routines and libraries of routines covering a wide range of disciplines, this program has become as ubiquitous as the calculator.

Instruction—During and After the Lecture

There are a number of notable applications of computers in technical courses on campus. The following examples illustrate the use of computer technology in the classroom as a means of enhancing student-teacher communication and as a method of providing individualized instruction and testing outside the classroom.

Professor Jeffrey Kantor, in the Department of Chemical Engineering, uses Mosaic, a platform-independent hypermedia program, to enhance the information and communication available to his students outside the classroom. Mosaic, which is available in the public clusters on campus, provides a uniform hypermedia interface across the Internet for many protocols, including Gopher, telnet, and email. It can display text, graphical data, images, and sound in a variety of common formats. Kantor uses Mosaic to make his lecture notes and numerous other items of information available to his students outside the classroom. "Course materials are not static," says Kantor. "This is an improvement upon paper. Notes can be updated more easily, and problems can be corrected quickly. In addition, it encourages email communication with students." As an example, when some of his students had trouble with a design, he was able to use Mosaic to provide a link to the University of Florida, where similar example designs are available. Platform independence is an important feature of the Mosaic software, said Kantor, because it allows any student with a computer and a network connection access to his course materials.

CScore, a program that can deliver and grade individualized assignments for students in a given class, as well as provide an on-line report of all their scores in the class, has been used to teach circuit theory in the Department of Electrical Engineering for the past three years. Based on an approach used throughout the 1980s to teach electrical network and system analysis by Dr. Michael K. Sain, Freimann Professor of Electrical Engineering, CScore was developed by the author. It can display text, numbers, and simple graphics, all of which can vary from student to student. The program allows students to work together on assignments but prevents explicit copying of the final answers; while the assignments are usually variations on the same theme, the intermediate and final answers differ from student to student. Furthermore, since students submit their answers to CScore for grading, feedback on the correctness of their solutions is immediate. Also, a central database keeps track of calls to the CScore program, allowing instructors to monitor progress.

Jim Johnson
Department of Chemistry

Computers have been used instructionally in the General Chemistry Laboratory curriculum since the fall semester of the 1982-83 academic year. Courseware was developed in-house for use on Apple II Plus computers, with a basic network providing centralized storage as well as automated access to programs by students. The obvious obsolescence of this original computer hardware, and more importantly the availability of the educational technologies of the DeBartolo Classroom building, provided dual incentives to improve and modernize the instructional use of computers in the laboratory course.

The General Chemistry Laboratory enrollment typically exceeds 800, necessitating several sections of lab each having a population of about 100. Our most recent courseware development goal was to create Macintosh replacements for the original Apple courseware and provide access by all laboratory students to these lessons using the Macintosh computers in the DeBartolo public cluster for the 1992-93 academic year. A tutorial format provided the fundamental structure for each lesson, which also included simulations, animations of concepts, and lab techniques. Authorware Professional was used initially as the development tool for these lessons, but was eventually replaced with HyperCard (which was initially more difficult but eventually more effective). Graphics and video development were completed primarily using SuperPaint, Photoshop, and Premiere, with Director used to create animations.

Supporting the tutorials was a glossary of chemical terms and a personalized notebook. Each term in the glossary, which was accessed from an alphabetized list, included a definition and, if appropriate, accompanying graphic. Additional features supported browsing, printing, viewing QuickTime movies, and contextual links to other terms in the glossary. The notebook also had similar features, and allowed the student to add pages of new terms, enter text, and copy/paste both text and graphics from the tutorials to the notebook. The notebook was a HyperCard stack residing on a floppy disk and was designed to be used on any Macintosh independent of the courseware or campus network.

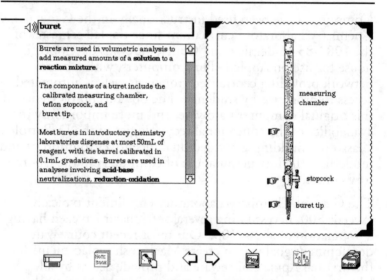

Figure 1. Entry from the Glossary

These tutorial lessons were designed for specific laboratory experiments, with the courseware completed prior to the experiment. A quiz over the courseware was given at the start of the laboratory period and was counted as part of the laboratory grade. Teaching assistants were available during each afternoon in the DeBartolo public cluster, providing assistance not only with questions concerning chemistry but also any usage problems involving the courseware. Although each courseware lessons had to reside on individual

Macintosh workstations, student tracking was maintained in centralized files. The purpose of these tracking files was to provide assistance in improving the courseware, although the manipulation of this large amount of data proved extremely cumbersome.

Student feedback through questionnaires clearly favored continued use of the courseware in the laboratory curriculum, although average quiz scores were lower than expected. Since a new lab curriculum has been implemented during the current 1993-94 academic year, new courseware is currently being developed or acquired for these new experiments. This courseware will be tool-oriented (with less emphasis on the tutorial format), require concurrent completion of worksheets (which will be part of the lab grade), with encouragement of peer collaboration. The MassSpecTool is an example of a HyperCard stack used to study chemical isotopes and mass spectra, and was first used during the 1993 fall semester.

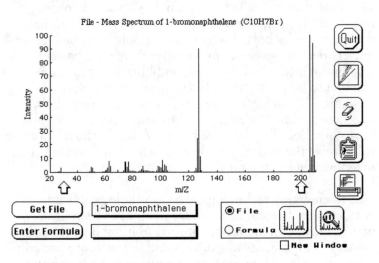

Figure 2. MassSpecTool

Barry Keating
Jesse H. Jones Professor
College of Business Administration

New Modes of Teaching in the Notre Dame
College of Business Administration

The current faculty in American universities have grown up and studied in an era in which scholarship and knowledge rested on the printed word; this is not very different than the concept of scholarship that was prevalent in the medieval universities. In medieval universities there were books to read, written tests to be graded, and libraries of printed material to be researched. Today, however, the electronic revolution has brought scholarship a new dimension. We may even see the beginning of the dominance of electronic forms of scholarship because most scholars in the near future will receive the majority of their information electronically; the same will be true for their students.

Due to emerging technology, the "psychological bandwidth" of teaching is becoming far wider than it has been in the past. Teachers are no longer limited to using only the print media in assignments to students and in classroom presentations. Visuals, animations, and simulations are becoming commonplace in courses in areas as widespread as statistics, accounting and economics. The new modalities are not just instances of "paving the cowpaths" of instruction by redoing old lecture notes and assignments with a word processor. This "second industrial revolution" as Nobel Laureate

28

Herbert Simon called it, is being used to forge higher levels of cognitive skills in a variety of ways.

What are these new modalities and how are they being applied to higher education? In one sense there is nothing new in our capabilities; we have had access to visuals, motion pictures, and sounds for some time. When a computer mediates the presentation, however, there is a difference; all the symbolics are present at the same time, together, in nonlinear form, and easily done. Information can be transformed from one symbol to another; tables of numbers may become graphics or a policy decision imputed as numbers may be translated into economic outcomes represented by tables and charts. Linkages that were difficult to draw in the past become easy to demonstrate; a discussion of price elasticity, for example, now may embody an animation demonstrating precisely how elasticities change with variations in the environment.

The most important change in the psychological bandwidth occurs when students move from reception to engagement. Students have been passive in the classroom throughout most of their careers. Simon calls most standard lecture experiences "learning by infection." The student absorbs some of what the instructor throws towards the students. With the addition of technology to DeBartolo Hall classrooms that has changed. Students are slowly moving away from passive reception towards active engagement in the learning process.

Most of the innovative DeBartolo classroom tools support what could be termed collaborative learning experiences in which students take active roles; the teacher becomes a mentor rather than a lecturer. Often the problem solving that takes place engages the teacher and more than one student in a collaborative effort. This is new ground for most faculty; to incorporate technology into a course requires designing the course from the ground up or a major redesign of an existing course. Such a redesign also assumes that there will be hardware, software, other technical support and some reward system for the effort. Two types of innovation being used in DeBartolo are particularly interesting: simulation and enhancements to traditional lectures.

Simulations

Simulation is a tool that has clearly benefitted from the electronic revolution. The technique is not new, but the inexpensive and effective implementation of the tool are new developments. Simulation is simply the difference between riding in an airplane and being the pilot.

Business and economic simulations have been around since the middle 1950s when the American Management Association published their "Top Management Decision Simulation" which allowed participants to play the role of top administrators in an organization. Simulations were a breakthrough in the learning process because they forced students to go from passive recipients of knowledge to active participants in a process. Not only did the instructor teach students, but students now taught each other as well. The structure of the simulation differed from older case studies because of the level of interaction and the ongoing sequences of decisions and consequences. Students now had to live with the results of their own decisions. But the early business simulations were awkward and cumbersome with calculations done by hand and lengthy amounts of time between decisions and results.

Computers allow virtually instantaneous calculation and DeBartolo Hall allows portability to the classroom. Several business economics instructors in the College of Business now simulate an entire economy (the U.S. economy) in the classroom in real time. The model used is commercially available (the Fair Model, designed by Professor Ray Fair of Yale University) and easily implemented by both students and faculty.

Models are nothing new to economists. They have often been presented to students as sets of equations which describe various sectors of the economy. Students were told that the model, when solved interactively, could describe what happens to employment and personal income if, for instance, the federal government imposes a 1 percent increase in the personal income tax. What is new about the manner in which the Fair Model is used today is that it can be an interactive part of the lecture.

As various policy actions are discussed and explained in the class, actual economic data (preloaded into the model) is used to calculate and report the results on a wide variety of economic variables. Students use the same model themselves in the DeBartolo Computer Cluster (or on their personal computers) when exploring their own "what if" types of questions. The active participation of the students may be the key to the effective use of simulation. Students not only rerun the simulation with different policy actions but, more importantly, re-estimate the parameters of the model. This active learning experience demonstrates in a first-hand manner how real-world economists produce forecasts and learn about economic relationships.

A very different type of simulation is used in the microeconomics courses in the College of Business. This simulation (called the Walrasian Simulator) is a straightforward representation of a buyer-seller auction-trading process, the kind of process which characterizes much of what we know as the market economy. It is not a complete, exhaustive representation of any particular market, yet, in a single 75 minute class this exercise permits students to experience some rather technical, but important, economic concepts such as elasticity and convergence towards equilibrium.

The conditions represented in the simulation are modeled closely upon the supply and demand curves generated by limit price orders in the hands of stock and commodity market brokers at the opening of any trading day in any one stock or commodity (e.g., the Chicago Board of Trade market in soybeans or the New York Stock Exchange market for IBM shares). One important feature of this simulation is the ease with which the instructor may change the initial conditions in order to demonstrate any number of economic phenomena. The simulation may then be thought of as a shell for use by instructors in explaining whatever market phenomena they choose to demonstrate.

The DeBartolo large screen projection is essential for the simulation because it substitutes for the perfect information assumption of the model. Students, by glancing at the screen during the simulated trading, may see the prices and quantities agreed to by their counterparts.

Since the information on trading is collected by the computer during the actual trading, it is a simple matter to calculate the desired trading statistics and display the results graphically at the end of the class period during the student debriefing.

Market Data: Day 1 thru Day 10

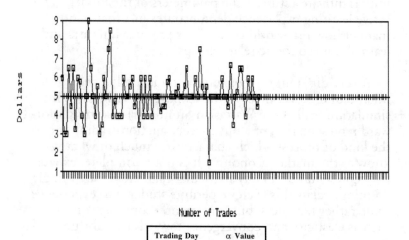

Trading Day	α Value
1	29.83287
2	33.37497
3	33.94849
4	17.60682
5	15.7233
6	10.84551
7	13.43503
8	23.5681
9	17.33494
10	15.63472

Note: The alpha values are the coefficients of convergence

Figure 1: This is an example of the summary projection used with the Walrasian Simulator during the end-of-class debriefing. The graph and statistics are calculated from the action of the students during the trading activity in that class.

"Traditional" Lectures

Not all classroom experiences are going to take the form of experiential or participatory learning such as simulation. There may be no substitute for the directed insight of a skilled scholar leading a class through a lecture in which any discussion is dominated by the instructor. But even here the electronic media and technological innovation are having an impact.

Lectures in the College of Business at Notre Dame are taking advantage of nontraditional tools. Some instructors are using computers in the classrooms as electronic blackboards in much the same ways they have always used blackboards. These instructors use HyperCard on the Macintosh or ToolBook on DOS/Windows machines to structure their presentations in a manner similar to the use of overhead transparencies.

The difference between the electronic blackboard approach and the traditional lecture with overheads approach is that the range of items the instructor uses on the projection again changes the psychological bandwidth. Not only is printed material in the form of "bullet points" or outlines available, but animations, moving graphics, and sound and video clips are also available in a manner easily accessed. Our economics instructors use displays of probability surfaces and three-dimensional representations of regression surfaces to demonstrate statistical properties that have been known for over 200 years. Is the electronic demonstration any better than a "straight lecture"?

Many of us believe the electronic enhancements make the material easier for students to interpret. These enhancements are not simply a different way of doing things but represent a better way of presenting material. We are providing students with views of our material which printed material and the ordinary lecture cannot provide. There is no way in which a three-dimensional economic production surface can be displayed and rotated in a transparency, a lecture or a book. But it is easy to do with a computer display. And once seen, it is simple to explain to students the difficult concepts, for example, of returns to scale and returns to a variable input.

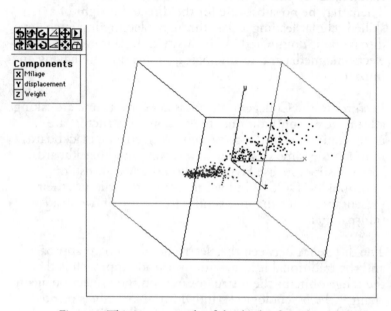

Figure 2: This is an example of the display for a dataset which includes three pieces of data for 192 actual automobiles: mileage, weight, and displacement. The display can be rotated using the controls in the upper left.

Lawrence C. Marsh
Department of Economics

This course is required for all students majoring in economics at Notre Dame. It is a statistics course which traditionally would have made extensive use of blackboard and chalk. However, no chalk or blackboard is now used in this course since all lectures from the first class day to the last class day are multimedia presentations. Although a couple of separate films provided by the American Statistical Association are used in the course, most of the materials presented are imported into Microsoft's PowerPoint 3.0 and presented as color lectures. This involves the importing of graphs and charts from Excel and MSGraph as well as equations from Equation Editor and Expressionist. QuickTime movies created in Cinemation and Theorist are also available to make the statistical concepts and methods clear.

1. In this class the professor and students do not spend valuable class time copying material onto a blackboard and transcribing it to notebooks. Instead handouts are generated automatically by PowerPoint with twelve slides per page (six-per-side back-to-back) and range from three pages for a 36 slide lecture to five pages for a 60 slide lecture. These are photocopied and made available to the students. This not only saves a great deal of class time enabling the professor to go into more detail and explain concepts more carefully, but it also ensures the accuracy of the equations, graphs, etc. in the notes that the students have. The slides are numbered so student's can easily ask questions about specific slides.

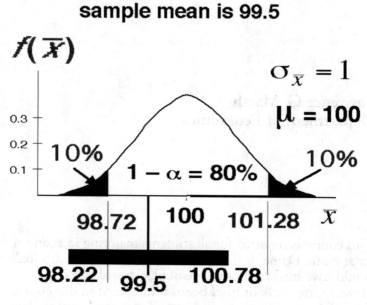

sample mean is 99.5

$f(\overline{x})$

$\sigma_{\overline{x}} = 1$

$\mu = 100$

0.3

0.2   **10%**

0.1 $1 - \alpha = 80\%$ **10%**

98.72   100   101.28 $\overline{x}$

98.22   99.5   100.78

Figure 1

2. During the lecture the professor uses the mouse to write directly onto the slides as they are being presented: circling important points, drawing arrows to emphasize relationships, and adding additional notes and comments "on the fly". When the professor needs more room to answer a question, he hits a "w" which brings up a white screen upon which he writes freely to answer the student's question. During the lecture when a student asks about a particular slide the professor just types the slide number and hits return to move directly to the desired slide. He uses transition effects in moving from slide to slide and makes use of the build function to display lines one at a time on a slide to discuss each point before bringing in the next one.

3. The Adventures in Statistics homework program gives DeBartolo computer lab assignments to the students that are due twice a week and is controlled over the network by the professor via Quant System's Classroom Management System. The Adventures program provides twenty-two homework assignments each of which consists of fifteen

questions. In order to get certified on a particular homework assignment, a student must answer at least thirteen of the fifteen questions for the assignment correctly. The numbers are randomized so that two students sitting next to one another face the same questions but a different set of numbers. The questions are not multiple choice. The students work out the answers with paper, pencil and a hand calculator and type their answers into the computer. Students may attempt certification on a particular homework as many times as necessary to achieve certification. Thus, sloppy or incomplete homeworks are not "turned in" because the computer program will not accept them. The Adventures program provides students with detailed help (diagrams, formulas, calculations, and explanations) in practice mode. When a student is ready to attempt certification, she switches to certification mode where no help is provided unless an incorrect answer is given. The computer program explains the student's error in detail showing with diagrams and explanation how to carry out the correct calculations to answer the question.

7. Consider the following data regarding world populations and land areas. [Population Reference Bureau, Inc]

Area	Estimated Population mid-1992 (in millions)	Approximate Land Area (sq. mile) (in millions)
Asia	3,207	10.6
Africa	654	11.7
North America	436	9.4
South America	300	6.9
Antartica	0	6
Europe	511	1.9
Oceania	28	3.3
U.S.S.R.	284	8.6

a. Plot the data points on a scatterplot.
b. Determine the correlation coefficient.
c. Describe the relationship indicated by the correlation coefficient and the scatterplot.

Discovering Statistics, James Hawkes

Figure 2

4. All students in this class are required to be active in e-mail. This is necessary so that they can receive the 30-digit letter-number code combination required for them to run the Adventures in Statistics computer homework program. E-mail also serves as a way of immediately transmitting messages to the professor regarding any aspect of the course. Students may call the professor at any time night or day at work or home to discuss statistics, but e-mail is useful when the professor is busy teaching another class or at committee meetings. When the answer to a question is pertinent to all students it is transmitted to the entire class using the electronic class list from the Registrar, the same class list used to create the electronic grade book for the course.

Michael N. Morris and Ramachandran Ramanan
Department of Accountancy

The Use of Educational Technology in Accounting 380

Quantitative Methods in Accounting (Accounting 380) is an applied statistics course that junior accounting majors in the College of Business are required to take. The course covers a variety of models that can provide assistance to decision makers either because the underlying problems are too complex or involve situations of a repetitive nature. Topics covered include decision analysis and information value, statistical sampling, regression, linear programming, and inventory models among others. Since the intuition underlying most of these models can best be explained by means of graphical images, we applied to the Jump-Start Grant Program through Educational Technology to get assistance. Our proposal was accepted.

Following discussions with Joe Williams and Tom Laughner, Office of University Computing, it was suggested that we pursue the use of software called Toolbook. This software helps in creating the graphical images and providing animation to visually display how optimization techniques arrive at solutions. We decided on developing four modules initially, including linear programming, regression analysis, bayesian revision in decision analysis, and inventory models. Some of these modules deal with deterministic and some with stochastic models.

39

The total package now consists of about 73 pages in Toolbook, portions of which are called up during lectures to enhance the discussion of the topics. Many of the images have hot buttons which pop up hidden text or initiate animation. Animation is useful in demonstrating how a technique works and in addressing sensitivity of a solution to changes in the input parameters.

The linear programming module constructs a feasible region for a problem with two decision variables, and animates the movement of the objective function through the feasible region to the optimal solution. Animation is also used to demonstrate sensitivity analysis for changes to both the objective function and constraints. The module on regression analysis graphically depicts the meaning of least squares and provides a host of data images showing violation of the assumptions of regression analysis. The Bayesian revision module presents a series of Venn diagrams which helps the student to visually observe the revision process from prior to posterior probabilities. The final module on inventory demonstrates the effect of stochastic demand (through animation) on the basic economic order quantity.

While initially developed for the spring of 1993, the modules have now been used for three semesters. In the spring of 1993 and 1994, the materials were used in DeBartolo Hall. In the fall of 1993, the modules were employed in the Study Abroad Program in Australia. In all of these presentations, it was truly satisfying to us that more students understood the intuition underlying these quantitative techniques with the graphical presentation. This understanding led to more critical thinking and discussion of "what if" situations in a more efficient manner.

Learning the intricacies of Toolbook in developing the four modules has given us the confidence to generate additional pages for daily lectures in the course. We currently have 16 additional Toolbook pages that are employed in the classroom to assist with lectures or to initiate discussion. We feel we are now equipped to develop Toolbook pages to enhance classroom learning in future teaching assignments.

In addition to the use of Toolbook, we employ spreadsheets and statistical software that accompanies the text in class. Calling up spreadsheets, which have been constructed prior to class, allows for efficient use of class time in further investigation of sensitivity analysis in homework and case problem solutions. DeBartolo Hall classrooms also allow access to the file server that students access in the workstation clusters. Using software in class with the exact menus and same versions of software as the clusters makes it less problematic for students to access the software outside of class. It also provides consistency for faculty and students on classroom and homework assignments and goes a long way towards minimizing students' fear of computers and technology.

John Halloran
Department of Finance

Experience in Using DeBartolo Hall Technologies

Prior to the availability of DeBartolo Hall, my experience with computer and media technologies involved the occasional use of videotapes in the classroom and a computer simulation of the financial management of a commerical bank. The simulation, which is an integral part of Commercial Bank Management (FIN 474), requires student teams to make a broad range of financial decisions comparable to those made by managers of real banks. The teams meet outside of class and make weekly decisions over most of the semester. These decisions are then processed by the computer which produces a ten page printout that contains financial statements and other indicators of the team's performance.

The simulation comes with a student manual that describes the basic rules and decision-making mechanics associated with the game. It provides very little insight, however, into bank financial analysis which is the major role of the simulation in my class. Consequently, I have developed a decision guide for the students that outlines bank financial analysis in the form of a series of lecture outlines. While the students have found this decision guide helpful in managing their banks, they sometimes express the desire for text to amplify and explain the lecture notes.

The Office of University Computing's workshop on technologies available in DeBartolo Hall revealed how computer technologies could be used to develop computer materials in connection with the computer simulation. The advantages of this electronic pedagogy were readily apparent in the course software demonstrated at the workshop. Material could be presented in a visually exciting and intellectually stimulating fashion. Hypermedia software could combine and integrate text, graphics, animation, video and audio material into one easily accessible package for the students. Thus, materials could be gathered and adapted from a much larger variety of sources than would normally be available to the students. In addition, the materials could be presented in an interactive fashion that encourages student participation and facilitates learning.

Over the last two years, I have used Toolbook authoring software to develop two types of materials in association with the bank simulation. First, I constructed a set of computer slides that summarize the materials contained in the decision guide (Figure 1). I use these slides in my classroom lectures on the simulation. Second, I have developed an electronic simulation decision guide for use by the students outside the classroom (Figure 2).

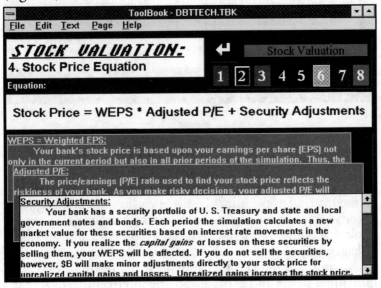

Figure 1

Development of the slides has forced me to carefully reconsider the important relationships in the simulation. The process of learning the capabilities and limitations of the software has enabled me to develop new ways of presenting the material. For example, each slide can only contain a limited amount of information. Thus, I was often forced to break a complicated page of outline notes into a series of much simpler and more visually appealing slides. The net result has been an improvement in student interest and ability to follow the classroom discussion of the decision guide.

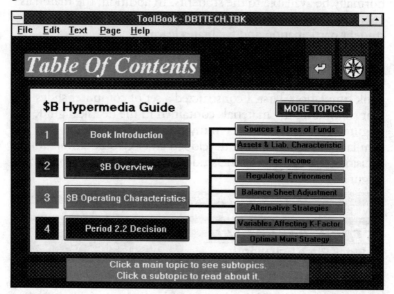

Figure 2

The development of the electronic decision guide has also posed pedagogical challenges. Instead of trying to condense material, the challenge has been how to expand and elaborate on the material in the most visually appealing and pedagogically effective way. I have organized the presentation as a hypertext book that allows nonsequential access to topics and provides linkages among various subjects. Through the use of extensive menus and indices, the students can quickly access individual topics and explore variable interrelationships that would not be so readily apparent in conventional printed materials. In addition, the use of submenus and pop-up fields enables the student to explore the material at the desired level. Material that has been mastered can be quickly reviewed at a general level.

Material that is not so well understood can be explored in a number of increasingly detailed levels of discussion. The development of this electronic decision guide has also helped me to rethink the most effective manner of discussing the simulation in the classroom. Since the students now have access to a detailed explanation of the simulation outside of class, I can cover the simulation in the classroom at a more general level and devote more class time to other topics.

My recommendation to faculty interested in the application of computer technology to their courses is to explore existing course software to develop an appreciation for the different pedagogical approaches currently in use. Such an exploration will provide insight into how computer technologies might be adapted to a specific course. Once the decision to adopt this electronic pedagogy has been made, be prepared to invest a large amount of time in two tasks. First, you must familiarize yourself with a specific software package so that you thoroughly understand its advantages and limitations. Second, you must convert conventional course materials into an electronic presentation format. The accomplishment of this conversion in a creative and effective manner is usually more difficult than initially anticipated.

Kern R. Trembath
Assistant Chairperson
Department of Theology

I began teaching the Foundations of Theology course 12 years ago when I was still a graduate student at the University of Notre Dame. Because this is a University-required course, between 20 and 25 sections are taught each semester. With such a large number of sections, but a rather finite number of maps and images to use in them, I wondered even back then how we might be able to harness technology to collect into one location everything that any teacher might ever wish to use. Each of us would then be benefited by having rapid access to what we individually wanted, but in addition by seeing what our colleagues were using.

The approach of DeBartolo Hall motivated me to pay more attention to this idea. My first attempt resulted in a very structured presentation model which demanded that the teacher list all of the images needed during the semester in a specified order, and then not deviate from that order in class. Joe Williams of the Office of University Computing encouraged to change from that model to one that allowed for much greater spontaneity and flexibility in class. He then enlisted others in the creation of the necessary software. At the moment, there are several professors using it, both in various departments here at Notre Dame and at other colleges as well. In addition to showing maps and pictures, it also allows me to display biblical and other texts, and to unpack arguments on the screen in ways that not only demonstrate them, but display their rhetorical structure as well.

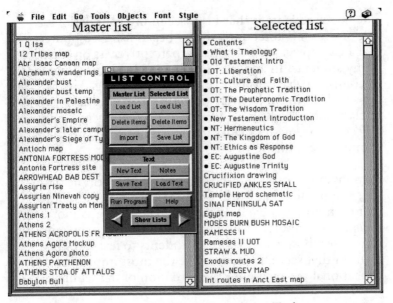

Figure 1. Text/Image Presentation Tool

The comfortable way in which Debartolo displayed the use of instructional technology produced another interesting variation. During the first semester that I used computers in class, I was asked a question one day that was both intrinsically interesting but also beyond the possibilities of a first-year introductory course. I opened the matter to all who were interested, and 6 of us signed on. We defined and divided the overall task, and then took some weeks off to pursue our individual assignments. During that time I opened my workstation to the campus network and invited the students to store their findings (notes, bibliographies, drafts, etc.) on it. My original intention was to read each draft and comment on it, much as I would have using traditional paper formats. What I discovered to my great delight, though, was that they took this function away from me; when student A uploaded material to my disk, students B & C read it on their screens and made comments based in their own research. This generated both much greater, and much more rapid, critical progress than any other structure of which I am aware, and produced a final product that was easily on a par with what we expect majors to accomplish.

The major advantage that I can see in my Foundations sections from before, until after, I began using computers is that I can now anticipate greater perceptiveness on the part of my students. In addition to enhancing my teaching, that is, computers have also enhanced their learning. This is detectable both subjectively (in terms of greater attentiveness in class, more "light bulb" reactions on their faces) and objectively (semester grades improved noticeably in the post-computer sections).

I am looking forward to the completion of dorm networking, and predict that it will produce learning innovations that even now, a mere 2-3 years in advance, we cannot imagine. Computer technology gives each of us the opportunity to test how much we trust students to learn on their own. In that sense, it may well be the most important educational advance since the invention of the seminar.

Eugene Ulrich
Department of Theology

This past Fall, I taught the Theology Foundations course
(THEO 100) in DeBartolo Hall to a class of 50 freshmen. In
the dozen years that I have been teaching this course, I have
projected 8.5 x 11 transparencies to convey lecture material.
My graduate assistant had already computerized these
transparencies from their original hand-written form in order
to create clearer, type-written overheads for the students. It
seemed a small and obvious step to project directly from the
computer disk. It was much easier, after all, to carry a disk to
class than a folder of slippery overheads, and I found it easier
to manipulate and navigate through computerized material
than to do so with separate sheets of plastic. Beyond these
pragmatic concerns, I am committed to incorporating
computers in my classes because I am so immersed in computer technology in my own research and because I am
convinced of the computer's ability to facilitate learning for
today's media-sophisticated students.

Kern Trembath, Assistant Chair of the Theology Department, provided further incentive to computerize: he had
created an optical disk with digitized diagrams, maps and
photographs pertaining to the Foundations course. I envi-
sioned teaching from my Microsoft Word lecture file and
periodically tapping in to the optical disk for visual material.

I also took advantage of the campus network's courseware
server to avail students of projected notes in a permanent file
accessible from any campus cluster.

Course preparation time was necessarily greater than Fall semester. First, I had to crop my lecture notes to the size of the computer screen. Notes that formerly fit on an 8.5 x 11 sheet had to be reduced to the 8.5 x 6 size of the projected image. Secondly, I had to condense course notes for the campus network courseware server. I anticipated that students would want to print the material, and I wanted to reduce the number of pages they would be printing. Throughout the term, I had to revise this material as my lectures diverged from my original plan and as student interest dictated new topics of discussion. Finally, I had to familiarize myself with the DeBartolo Hall facilities and the optical drive technology. The technical staff in DeBartolo trained me to run the equipment at the beginning of the term and were always available to respond to malfunctions. The optical drive technology was more difficult to master. I spent a good amount of time choosing a list of images to project, but had little time to practice making smooth transitions between lecture notes and optical images. Fearing that the flow of class would be interrupted, I rarely utilized this resource.

The most effective pedagogical tool by far was the network courseware server. Students had permanent access to lecture notes, which theoretically enabled them to spend less time writing and more time learning in class. Because DeBartolo Hall is connected to the network, I was able to demonstrate use of the courseware server in class. Two-thirds of the class were MAC users; nevertheless, almost all used the courseware server and found it helpful. Attendance was not perceptibly affected by the availability of class notes.

Teaching from the computer was generally effective. Transitions between topics were smoother and material corresponding to random student questions was easier to locate. Effectiveness was occasionally hampered by equipment failures, however. In my classroom, a laptop and optical disk drive had to be installed prior to each class. While the consultants were always highly cooperative, the laptop's labyrinthine wiring was not. If one wire was dislodged before class, a consultant had to be summoned and class was late starting. In anticipation of such glitches, I found it helpful to have on hand a compete set of overhead transparencies corresponding to my computerized lecture notes.

I plan to develop my technological facility before I teach the course again next Fall. I am particularly interested in practicing with the optical disk and in converting my Courseware server into an interactive, multi-media format accessible from any platform on campus. I have just two recommendations for other faculty interested in classroom technology. First, be reasonable as you anticipate your technology goals for each term. You may not be able to do everything you want all at once! Second, allocate plenty of time during your slower terms to learn to use the equipment, the facilities, and the software you choose. Effectiveness is enhanced if your materials are well-prepared and if your use of the equipment in class seems to be "second-nature."

Jeff VanderWilt
Department of Theology

I approached Joe Williams and Tom Laughner, Educational Technology Consultants for the Office of University Computing (OUC) at Notre Dame, in August of 1993. I was chomping at the bit to use all the "bells and whistles" which would soon be at my disposal in Notre Dame's new classroom building, DeBartolo Hall. Fresh in the classroom, fresh in the building, a new course. I wanted to start on the right foot. And, to be quite honest, my immediate desire was to avoid the time and expense of overhead transparencies and slides. I knew I could not afford them.

I was encouraged to write a proposal for a "Jump Start" grant offered by the OUC and the Department of Educational Media. In my proposal I requested a copy of Microsoft (MS) Powerpoint for Windows. Additionally, Prof. Kern Trembath of the Department of Theology had compiled a substantial library of images pertinent to Theology 100, the course I would be teaching. However, Kern's images are all stored in Macintosh format. Since I intended to use MS Windows at home and at school, I asked for help through the grant proposal in transferring selected images from Kern's library into Windows bitmaps.

I have now used Powerpoint for Windows and selected images during almost all of my lectures in Theology 100. This semester, Spring 1994, I was too late to reserve a classroom with a DOS/Windows computer for my class period. I was one of the last professors in my time slot to reserve a Macintosh Powerbook. Loading Powerpoint for Windows files on the Powerbook has caused fortunately few difficulties. I have recently ordered a PC utility which will allow me to save and format Macintosh diskettes from my PC at home. This should save time since I should then be able to load my lecture/presentations directly into the Powerbook at the beginning of each class.

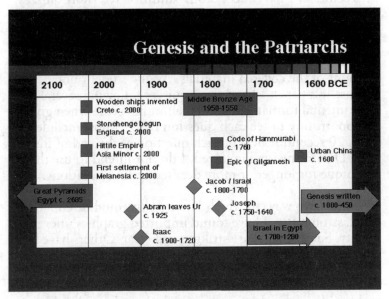

Figure 1. Genesis Timeline

Using Powerpoint in the classroom has several advantages. Powerpoint is best suited for a "uni-directional" flow of information. When I am presenting factual and visual information to students for the first time, Powerpoint is an effective tool for capturing their attention and for reinforcing the information I choose to present in class. Several types of slides work particularly well in this context. Timelines, maps, lecture outlines, and visual images have been particularly effective. I am particularly fond of several paintings by Rembrandt on biblical characters. For example, I embedded a scan of Rembrandt's painting of Jeremiah lamenting Jerusalem in the lecture/presentation on the Babylonian exile. This added an affective dimension to our discussion of the exile which words alone could not have conveyed. Timelines have helped students visualize temporal and historical relationships among the periods and persons we have studied. Short quotes, lecture outlines, and technical terms displayed on-screen help students feel secure with the material I am presenting.

This semester I have successfully administered short quizzes directly from the video screen. Powerpoint features automatically timed presentations. I have given students from one to two minutes per question. This allows greater flexibility than photocopied quizzes. And, I can make "up to the minute" revisions of the covered materials. As one student noted, we also use less paper. I have given quizzes following several experimental formats. Students felt most secure when given an opportunity to see each question twice. I now include a 15 to 20 second review of each question at the end of the quiz. Due to the time involved, I do not intend to use this technique for longer or more detailed testing situations.

I imagine two ways in which Powerpoint could be enhanced for classroom use. I have found imported graphics uneven in quality. Some images are striking and clear. Others have been embarrasingly dark or grainy. Some images scale to size quite easily. Others, I sense, could fill the whole screen and still be dissatisfying. Where I had hoped a map would appear crisp and legibly in the classroom, it might have been illegible. MicroSoft Windows bitmaps are difficult to edit, yet other image standards (.JPG, .PCX, .GIF) are either not supported in Powerpoint or are not well-suited to 256-color graphics (e.g., .PCX).

Powerpoint, I suggest, could embrace a more "bi-directional" model of communication. Powerpoint presentations are most effective when information is conveyed in one direction, from presenter to audience. When information must be conveyed from the audience, my students, to presenter (and then back to the entire audience), Powerpoint falls flat. For classroom discussions, I often resort to the blackboard. I suggest that future revisions of Powerpoint might include a "blackboard" or "notepad" tool. On a Powerpoint "black-board" one might insert diagrams or sketches or on a "notepad" type additional, ad hoc text. One could incorporate new or newly revealed information on the spot into a lecture/presentation. If I could insert a "blackboard" object onto predetermined slides, I believe that student input into classroom discussion could more easily be elicited and visually validated.

As a novice instructor, I have found this use of classroom technology very helpful. To compose lectures in Powerpoint presentations has helped me remain organized and on target. Lectures have been more focused and less prone to wander. Students, I sense, have felt more confident in me and in the information I convey when it is also presented on screen. This raises several interesting questions. Is information somehow "more true" for my students when they see it on the screen at the same time that I say it? Does the "truth" of the video screen surpass, for them, the "truth" of the words I deliver in lecture? I am not insensitive to these problems. Perhaps technical glitches (slides out of order, fuzzy pictures and the like) are more important than they might seem. They effectively suspend my student's suspension of disbelief. They remind students that the material presented on screen is intrinsically no more reliable than any other information which we all bring with us to class.

Most important, electronic media has given me flexibility. While I have made many "learning curve" errors in my classroom, I have been able to quickly and easily adjust presentations to meet unforeseen needs and concerns. Since I am not bound up in hard-copy handouts and overhead transparencies or slides, I have been able to adjust for those difficulties with ease. A more successful course, I believe, has been the result.

Anne C. McGuire
Department of Theology

Introduction to Christian Liturgy:
A Multi-media Approach

The concept of utilizing various media to acquaint students with Christian Liturgy was a natural idea. Liturgy itself is basically multi-dimensional. The course is basically divided into two segments. The first is historical, the second is theological and contemporary. My approach to the historical section is to explore as many dimensions of the historical experiences of liturgy as are available. These include, but are not limited to, maps, architecture, music, vestments, vessels, orders of service, and books. The contemporary theology is more experiential, drawing on many of the same dimensions, but placing them in contexts which can be more immediate to the students' lives.

DeBartolo Hall classrooms are suited to a presentation format which incorporates images and texts together using a computer. The software I used was Powerpoint, a presentation program for the Mac. For each class period, I used Powerpoint to display images and texts, some together, some interspersed (see Figures). This was most useful for architectural spaces, where a picture or drawing of the exterior could be shown on the same slide as its blueprint, floorplan, or cross-section. As one period in Christian history was discussed, the class could be exposed to the spaces used for worship, the artifacts utilized by the ministers and the people, and the texts recited or sung. It was, in a sense, a combination of slides and overheads, but with a little more freedom than either offered alone.

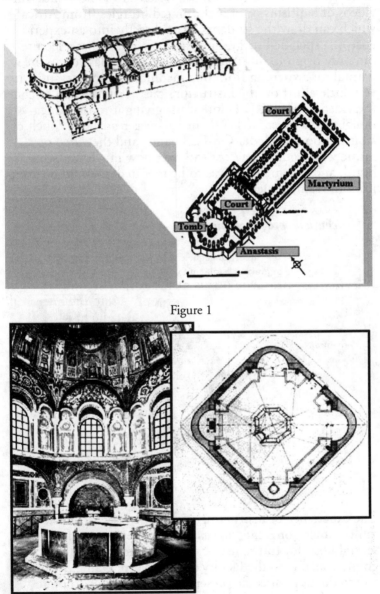

Figure 1

Figure 2

During the second part of the course, when contemporary expressions of worship are studied, music and videos are more available for classroom use. There are some wonderful videos of baptisms or of incluturated liturgies (from Africa) which can draw the students more directly into an experience of a specific liturgy, intensifying a point that a lecture can only begin to illustrate. The DeBartolo classrooms are a natural for switching from one medium to another, and with very little effort on the instructor's part. I simply had to cue the video, tape or CD before class, giving it to the educational media personnel. Whenever I was ready, one touch of a button on the Media-On-Call panel, and the video or music was begun. I had control over how much was seen or heard, and if something was to be repeated, it could be done from the same panel.

eucharistic prayer or anaphora

→*sursum corda* or preface dialogue
→ thanksgiving or preface, leading into
→ holy, holy (*sanctus*)
→ institution narrative
→ anamnesis
→ epiclesis
→ petitions
→ doxology and Amen

Syria 7th c

Figures 3 & 4

The experience of instructing with these very accessible multi-dimensional media was only the beginning, for I have several ideas for future use of the computer generated programs available to the faculty here at Notre Dame. I would like to develope specific presentations which incorporate maps with "hot spots," which could open on specific architectural spaces or landscapes, with further hot spots for close-ups, diagrams, etc. In addition, I would like to be able to incoporate music as a background to specific images. Then, when an Eastern Orthodox space, with its many icons, was being viewed on the screen, Orthodox chant could be playing over the speakers. These many possibilities only enhance the students' experience of, and therefore knowledge of, Christian liturgy, both its history and its current theology.

Edward A. Kline
Francis J. O'Malley Director
Freshman Writing Program

The Computerized Writing Process

Effective in the fall semester of 1992, all instructors of
English 109, "Composition and Literature," in the Freshman
Writing Program began supplementing their instruction in
writing with features of the Daedalus Integrated Writing
Environment, a series of programs designed to enhance and
reinforce each step of the writing process. After completing
one of two university-sponsored twelve-hour workshops
during the summer months, the instructors have introduced
approximately nine hundred students each semester to the
features of Daedalus. Periodic update technical sessions for
faculty occur during each semester.

In brief, the writing process without using a computer
consists of six steps: (1) prewriting activities such as choosing
a topic and planning the writing; (2) writing: various
freewriting techniques (brainstorming, clustering, outlining,
etc.); determining a sense of audience as well as purpose;
positing a preliminary thesis; producing a draft copy: (3)
responding: to one's own writing or to commentary on it
received from peers or one's instructor; reconsidering the
sense of audience and purpose; adjusting the thesis, as
appropriate; producing a second draft copy; (4) revising:
rethinking and reorganizing; making additions, deletions,
substitutions (not to be confused with editing); (5) editing:
checking grammar, punctuation, usage, format, spelling,

diction, sentence variety, paragraphing techniques, etc.; (6) evaluating: judging the quality of the final draft by oneself as well as by one's instructor. These steps do not necessarily follow in a linear fashion: the recursive nature of the process often interrupts the linear progression as when, for example, steps 3 and 4, responding and revising, can lead a writer back to step 2, writing, or even step 1, prewriting.

A writer does nothing with a computer that cannot be done without a computer: one simply does it more thoroughly and often more quickly with the use of the Daedalus system. How does one incorporate the Daedalus features into the steps of the writing process? Daedalus contains a word processing language called WRITE; however, it need not be used; Daedalus is compatible with three other word processing languages available on campus: ClarisWorks, WordPerfect, and Microsoft Word. Our teachers do not provide instruction in word processing: students must learn this skill on their own; nevertheless, a student may access WRITE or the other three processing languages named above on the server dedicated to the Freshman Writing Program (FWP) where the standard formatting procedures for papers submitted in the FWP will appear automatically.

The Invent, Respond, and InterChange functions of the Daedalus environment constitute the most frequently used features. Invent especially enhances the first two steps of the writing process: prewriting and writing. Students may select from the Invent feature the prompts based on Aristotle's "Topoi (topics)," Burke's "Pentad," a tagmemic matrix, narrative, poetry analysis, prose analysis, or any of approximately one hundred specialized and specific invention prompts authored by teachers of the composition-literature course. The respond prompts, used in steps three and four of the writing process, provide students with choices for local revision, global revision, narrative revision, or approximately eighty prompts designed by the faculty. The InterChange function becomes especially useful in conjunction with steps three and four. An interactive "discussion" feature, InterChange allows students to collaborate in pairs, trios, quartets, or any size group including the full class, with

61

several advantages over oral collaboration in the classroom: it is quieter, it draws into discussion "marginalized" students, and a printed record of the collaboration/discussion becomes available. Step five, editing, can be assisted through programs which activate spelling and grammar checks, concordance construction, thesaurus capabilities, word and sentence counts, etc. A unique feature of Daedalus, BiblioCite provides a painless and efficient methodology to cite bibliographical sources resulting in correctly presented citations in either MLA or APA formats.

Fortunately, Daedalus has no feature to correspond to the sixth step of the writing process: evaluation. The writer alone decides when to interrupt the writing process, whether after a fourth or fortieth draft, to submit it for evaluation by its intended audience, usually the teacher of the course. Here the Daedalus Delivery feature allows the student to electronically submit the essay to the teacher, the entire class, or both. However, since the fall semester of 1993, the students use the campus e-mail Eudora system for these purposes. Also contained in the Daedalus Environment are "User Help" and "Instructor Help" features which clearly explain the procedures to follow in order to activate any of the Daedalus functions.

An in-house evaluation instrument, administered each semester since Fall, 1992 reveals that over eighty percent of the students believe that they write better using the Daedalus system.

Jean A. Strebinger
Freshman Writing Program

Educational Technology and English 109

I have used the Media Resource Center and the university's computer network primarily for visual aids in teaching English 109, Composition and Literature. I did not need to use the Media-On-Call system to teach composition in English 109, because the Freshman Writing Program already has a computer-aided instruction program on the network. Like all teachers of English 109, too, I require students to submit some assignments through e-mail. In addition to the educational technologies available in the Freshman Writing Program, I have used the Media-On-Call for the literature in this course.

Before I explain my experience with the Media-On-Call system in DeBartolo, I need to explain how my approach to literature in English 109 led me to explore these educational technologies. I introduce literature through the theme, society, and the individual, because it provides a broad, humanistic approach and because it gives students something specific to look for while they read. I frequently bring in books relating to the society represented in the literature, and I often bookmark illustrations for reference during class. When we read, for example, the frequently anthologized selection "High Horse's Courting" from Black Elk Speaks, I passed around some books about the Plains Indians; after viewing pictures of daily life and acquainting ourselves with the role of the horse in this society, we discussed the story with a heightened awareness of its cultural context. These visual aids not only help to make students aware of the cultural context of literary works but also serve to entice many students (who are generally not English majors) to the pleasures of the written word. Though the students respond well to literature with the help of such visual aids, I find it burdensome to carry these heavy materials into class.

After a tour of the Media Resource Center in DeBartolo Hall, I realized that its educational technologies could help lift this burden and simplify my presentation through the use of still video, which records up to 50 images onto a 2" disk.. By copying pictures from books to these disks, I did not have to bring in books to class. The use of still video also simplified my presentations by allowing all students to view the pictures clearly and immediately. Last semester I made two still video disks, one for the Middle English poem "Sir Gawain and the Green Knight" and one for a Dickens' novel. The use of still video disks, however, did require more advanced planning than passing around books. I made an appointment with Mr. Claude Devaney in the Department of Educational Media, and it took us about 45 minutes to record 25 pictures. I also had to arrange for a time to show the images; and, because my class did not meet in DeBartolo Hall, I had to arrange with the Registrar for a room change. The still video disks, however, were well worth the extra planning and cost ($12.00 per disk). The pictures came out very clearly, and lively discussions followed the presentation.

In addition to still video, I also used the Media-On-Call system to show film adaptations of two plays that my class read. Though some students disagreed over the film's interpretation of the drama, I noticed that the videos helped the students visualize the drama and pay attention to props and other details that they missed in their readings.

As a result of my good experience with still video, I am currently working on a Macintosh-based presentation which uses scanned images. The presentation program offers more flexibility than still video, because I can rearrange pictures into different sequences for different lectures. However, I do miss the professional touch of the still videos. Some pictures come out very clearly, but others do not. Maps, for example, do not reproduce well on this program, and I may have to use an overhead for these. I understand that a professor may request aid for qualified students to scan these pictures; however, because I wanted to learn the program, I did not apply.

To date, I have found that the use of still video has been most successful in my English 109 class both because they offer an alternative method of presentation and because they help to lift the burden of transporting materials to class. For those teachers who would like to show computer scans of pictures, I would recommend asking for professional help in doing the scanning. Unless one is interested in exploring the computer world, scanning takes up time that might better be spent doing research.

James Dougherty
Department of English

I have taught three classes in DeBartolo Hall, all of them in the seminar rooms on the third floor that have a TV monitor for Media-On-Call. I have used Media-On-Call to present excerpts from videotapes. Students tend to nod off during extended video presentations, and since classroom instruction costs each Notre Dame undergraduate $22 an hour, I use only brief glimpses or single frames that will generate discussion. In the Arts and Letters Core Course, I used a video on Georgia O'Keeffe as a way of bringing into the classroom a sequence of her paintings—an alternative to slides, which are too costly to digitize for such infrequent use. The monitors are of such high quality that the images were perfectly clear, without lines or rolling: I asked the class to pair off and discuss what they saw for about five minutes, and then advanced to the next painting. Then the whole class shared their thoughts about O'Keeffe. Later in the year the Core Course saw *Boyz n the Hood*. The student discussion leaders in my section chose two 30-second sequences, each depicting an interaction between parents and children: after it played, the class discussed what they saw, played it again to confirm or challenge what they had said about it, re-argued it, and then played it as a finale. In a course on American poetry, I use a series of videotapes, each on a single poet, that was prepared for a PBS series a few years ago. The students are expected to view them outside class; but occasionally, when the videos have been especially ingenious in reproducing the images of a poem or in devising a graphic about its techniques, I call in clips from the video as a basis for discussion or new applications in the classroom. When thus restricted and applied to discussion, Media-On-Call's resources can enhance human interactive learning.

I have not used any of the other features of Media-On-Call, nor have I taught in one of the large lecture halls where more sophisticated programs are available. I think education requires performance by humans, not machines. Though I don't claim to be a successful performer, if I used one of the big classrooms I would have to learn how to apply these resources fluently and in ways subordinate to my own lecturing style, a mix of structure and improvisation. Because they are costly (in both money and time) to produce, such applications would have to be part of the permanent structure rather than the expendable improvisation.

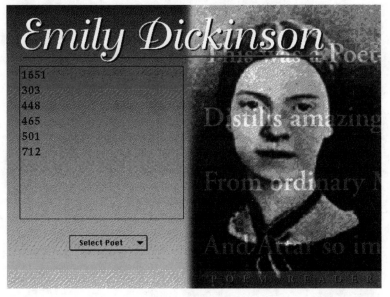

Figure 1. PoemReader

With abundant skillful assistance from the Office of University Computing, I am developing a Hypercard-based tutorial program, PoemReader, to help students gain the skills required to read poems well. Non-linear and self-paced, it is intended not for classroom use but for private instruction: before coming to a lecture on Emily Dickinson, the students are expected to work through the Dickinson poems in PoemReader. More advanced students learn a lot more about poetry by writing tutorials themselves, on Dickinson or some other poet, which then are added to the bank of what's available for beginners. These tutorials are available in the DeBartolo cluster, as they are elsewhere on campus. Thus far, my students have found them very helpful and often wish there were more of them not only for my courses but for other English courses as well.

Sandra Chrystal Hayes
Freshman Writing Program

Review of the DeBartolo Hall Technologies

For several years prior to DeBartolo Hall's resources, I frequently used an overhead projector in English 109 class, and I required all essays to be generated through a computer word-processing program. In order to assist the students, I usually required them to attend an introductory session in the computer room in O'Shaughnessy Hall and then encouraged them to take additional word processing classes.

Now the DeBartolo technological facilities improve the students' learning in my writing class and in my Freshman Seminar class. The computer system provides another form of communication, a vital pedogogical tool, which fosters the process approach to writing and stimulates critical thinking. The cluster/lab apparatus encourages lively idea exchange between students and me; the interactive learning improves their attention and response to assignments. Using e-mail and posting class assignments through the Daedalus system clarifies my expectations and assists when questions arise. E-mail tasks include posting assignments, transmitting essays and journals, and questioning assignments. Additionally, the Daedalus prompt series frames individual topics for the students' consideration. This software's prompt series aids students' analyses of a picture, other students' writing, and literature. The Interchange component structures small group conferences to discuss literature and to evaluate student papers. I project their class agenda or group conference on the two large screens in the lab. Word processing tools such as Grammatik and Spellcheck aid students' editing, while grammar diagnostics and lessons are provided through the Freshman Writing Program tutorial. Student conferences frequently include revising the student's paper on the computer in my office.

Two special projects for my Freshman Seminar, "Representations of Conflict: Gender, Racial, Religious, and International," grew out of the computer-based multimedia potential. The first entitled "No (Wo)men's Zone: German and American Women Artists, Writers, and Musicians in WWI", presents images originally created for slides, video, handouts, and textbook. Background music that I used to play on my children's jam box now plays through the computer-media mix.

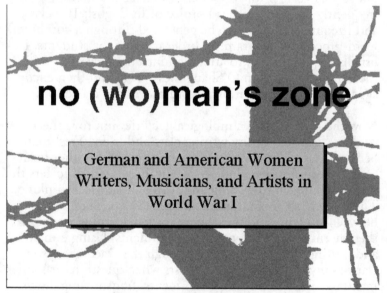

Figure 1. No (Wo) Man's Zone

Rather than ordering and carrying slides, projector, disc, video recorder, papers, and cassette player which I had previously done for class and for conferences, I now touch the mouse and generate the 75 minute presentation. In order to spur more active involvement, I require the students to open their electronic journals and to respond at three different times. After the presentation, they may review this lesson through the Coursework server on the computers in the clusters.

Dialogic History

Figure 2. No (Wo) Man's Zone

The second project grew out of my research on the first. One of the women writers, Mary Borden, wrote *The Forbidden Zone*, a book of essays and poems based on her experience as a nurse in France. Using Inter-Library Loan, I located a copy of the out-of-print edition, and decided to incorporate sections into the syllabus. Formerly, I would have duplicated and distributed these portions, but with Joe Williams' assistance and the use of the Voyager Electronic Book Toolkit, I was able to have the text scanned, to annotate lines or words that I wanted the students to note, to have the text available in the clusters, and then to compose computer follow-up questions. With this project, as well as with the former, I shall continue to add and to alter sections and assignments.

71

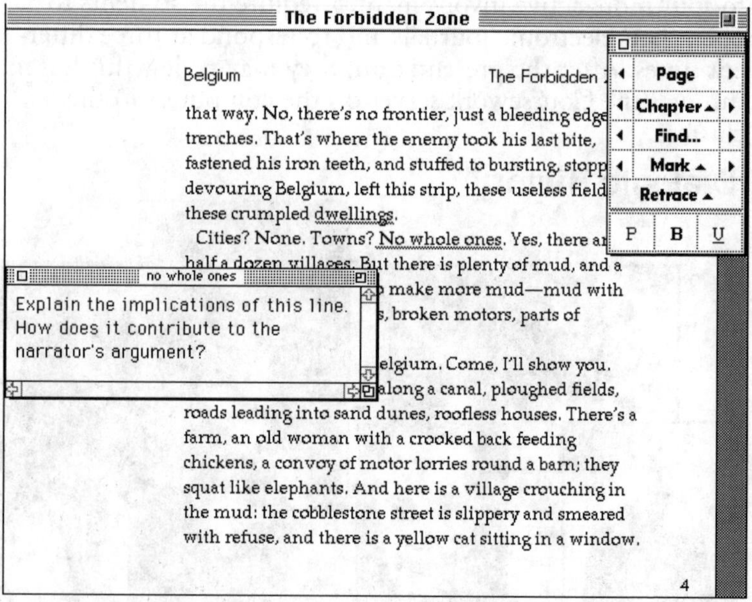

The Forbidden Zone

Belgium   The Forbidden

that way. No, there's no frontier, just a bleeding edge
trenches. That's where the enemy took his last bite,
fastened his iron teeth, and stuffed to bursting, stopp
devouring Belgium, left this strip, these useless field
these crumpled dwellings.

Cities? None. Towns? No whole ones. Yes, there ar
half a dozen villages. But there is plenty of mud, and a
make more mud—mud with
s, broken motors, parts of

Belgium. Come, I'll show you.
along a canal, ploughed fields,
roads leading into sand dunes, roofless houses. There's a
farm, an old woman with a crooked back feeding
chickens, a convoy of motor lorries round a barn; they
squat like elephants. And here is a village crouching in
the mud: the cobblestone street is slippery and smeared
with refuse, and there is a yellow cat sitting in a window.

no whole ones

Explain the implications of this line.
How does it contribute to the
narrator's argument?

| Page |
| Chapter |
| Find... |
| Mark |
| Retrace |
| P | B | U |

4

Figure 3. Electronic Version of Mary Borden's *The Forbidden Zone*

Student evaluations on the computer-based assignments and
computer-based multimedia project have consistently been
excellent, but an unexpected reward came to me recently.
Meeting with me to prepare for a class leadership role next
month, a student asked if she could design a computer/
multimedia presentation and use it in conjunction with her
discussion of a portion of Toni Morrison's *Sula*. Her enthusiasm and willingness to devote extra time to an assignment
marks another positive result of this DeBartolo Hall experience.

Edward A. Kline
Francis J. O'Malley
Director Freshman Writing Program

Becoming Persuasive

The use of Persuasion 2.1 allows presenters to abandon their overhead transparencies in the classroom and to replace them with professional-appearing "slides" operated from a lap top computer along with a LCD (liquid chrystal display) plate and controlled by clicking a mouse or keyboard spacebar. The Persuasion 2.1 program requires neither special programming knowledge nor special artistic/graphic skills: following instructions and simple good taste will suffice as one faces a palette of colors ranging from vibrant darks to shimmering pastels and a host of graphic selections from both within and outside of the program it self

Despite the advantages that accrue with the use of transparencies, fans of this enhancement of pedagogy will agree that some unpleasantries ensue. Unless one's transparencies are professionally produced, which can become quite expensive, the resultant product has an amateurish look. Most people lack the talent and skill to print letters evenly or consistently in a straight line with a uniform size. Unless one tapes the transparencies to a cardboard frame (another expense) or separates them with sheets of paper between them (which sometimes slip away), the transparencies stick together. Wetting the finger or thumb to separate the stuck-together transparencies often results in smearing the ink. Another nuisance factor resides in the overhead projector pens which invariably become misplaced. If the cap does not securely cover the pen point, the ink dries out. Layering presents another problem when the "barndoors" come loose, folded, or torn away. Additionally, with each presentation, the transparencies must be placed in the proper order. Because each transparency must be placed on the projector one at a time, whether framed or not, problems arise when they are dropped or become out of order. The distracting physical acts of manually changing the transparencies and turning the light on and off on the projector focus attention on the presenter, not the material presented.

The use of Persuasion 2.1 enables the presenter to overcome each of the problems inherent in using transparencies. All of the "slides" look professional. One can choose to work in color or in black/white, size choices for machine-generated text are legion, and the styles include: plain, bold, italic, underline, outline, shadow, superscript, and subscript. The presenter can select from a host of special effect options to highlight the text on the slide such as line styles (from thin to thick), line and fill patterns (39 choices), and shadow patterns (39 choices). Because the images are stored on disk, the presenter need not be concerned with stuck-together transparencies, dried-out pens, finger-smudged text, or dropping transparencies and getting them out of order. "Barn door" layering difficulties become simplified in the Persuasion 2.1 program which permits the presenter to design layer upon layer of materials, limited only by the choice of font size, the size of the screen, and practical concerns for the size of the room in which the presentation will be given. After all, one does want the text to be readable. For those presenters who have the skills, talents, or patience required, they can print their own text and/or draw their own graphics with the tools provided with the program.

To allow the presenter to provide visual variety to ward off monotony, Persuasion 2.1 incorporates a selection of graphics' categories and choices as listed: backgrounds: 7, borders/framers: 8, bullets/arrows: 19, communications/media: 16, financial: 11, maps: 5, message balloons: 9, people: 14, places: 4, time: 5, and transportation: 5. Or one can access the resources of Hypercard and import graphics from such series as "Art Bits," "Fred's Clip Art," and the like.

Where and when can one use Persuasion 2.1? Anywhere or any time one makes a presentation: in the classroom, at faculty meetings, in committee meetings, at off-campus conference presentations, honor code orientations, orientations for new faculty and teaching assistants, on-site visits to the computer classroom facilities in DeBartolo Hall. In fact this very essay could benefit by a Persuasion 2.1 presentation. Four sample frames follow from a presentation on the writing process which exemplify headers (the numbered entries), layering (each line of text appears on cue by clicking the mouse), graphics from the Persuasion 2.1 program (frames 1, 3, 4), and imported graphics from Hypercard (frame 3).

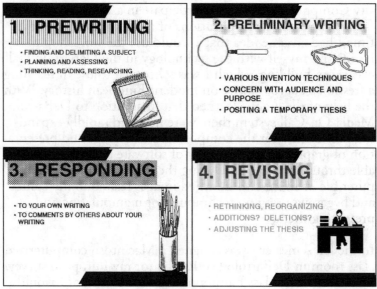

Figures 1-4

"To persuade" means to lead someone to "undertake a course of action or embrace a point of view by means of argument, reasoning, or entreaty" (*The American Heritage Dictionary*, 3rd ed., 1993, 1020). Achieving these goals with the use of Persuasion 2.1 is limited only by the mind of the presenter.

Thomas Kselman
Department of History

In the summer of 1993 I was awarded a small grant from the Department of Educational Media and the Office of University Computing (OUC) to participate in a workshop to train faculty in classroom applications of the computer. At the time I had a vague idea that I would use the workshop to familiarize myself with the technology in the DeBartolo Hall classroom building, which I was scheduled to use in teaching a freshman survey course on modern European history. With the help of the grant I learned that in addition to DeBartolo's Media-On-Call system there were new and rapidly expanding possibilities for the computer-based storage and presentation of graphics using a variety of software packages available through the OUC. During the summer I built a computer file of about two hundred images related to my course, and began working on techniques for manipulating and presenting them.

In the fall semester I was assigned a Macintosh computerized class room in DeBartolo (100 seats) for my European survey. During the first class I announced to students that I would be experimenting with the different possibilities available with the DeBartolo building and that occasionally there might be a few bugs in the system or my use of it. In succeeding classes I tried and generally succeeded in presenting at each lecture about ten still images, and one or two video segments to illustrate points I was making. For example, in talking about witchcraft in the sixteenth and seventeenth centuries, I showed through the Media-On-Call system a brief excerpt from Shakespeare's *Macbeth* as well as still images from my computer files of supposed witchcraft practices from sixteenth-century woodcuts. To illustrate the theme of romantic love I played an aria from a film version of Verdi's *La Traviata* and for a lecture on the youth culture of the 1960s I played the opening scene from *A Hard Day's Night* (I regret not handing out the course evaluations after this particular lecture.) For still images I relied heavily on a laser disc designed for European history courses that was purchased by the Department of Educational Media. With the help of the OUC staff I was able to capture these and transfer them to my own file, which made them easier to access. I also scanned some slides and illustrations from books, which I also stored in my master file.

In the course of the semester I also experimented with the presentation of textual material through the computer. By mid-semester I found that students appreciated having detailed outlines of the lecture displayed as they came into class and I also found it helpful at times to show a quotation that I had in my lecture notes, which they could read while I discussed and interpreted it. The outlines and quotes proved so useful that students asked that copies be made available to them. To do this I created a file on the courseware server, and explained to students how they could gain access to it. By the end of the semester they were using the outlines to prepare for tests, and one of my teaching assistants suggested that they had become "outline-dependent" which is probably a fair assessment.

I had somewhat less success in trying to integrate music into my presentations. Initially I had hoped to play music from the period while students entered the class, but found that I was unable to present an outline through the computer system and play music from Media-On-Call at the same time. This problem illustrates one difficulty I had throughout the semester, for in general I found it cumbersome trying to move back and forth between the computer and Media-On-Call. Student response to my experiments with the technologies available in DeBartolo Hall was generally positive. Despite the amount of time it took to learn and use the new technology (which was much more than I originally expected) I plan to continue using both Media-On-Call and the computerized classrooms of DeBartolo Hall.

Daniel Sheerin,
Department of Classical and Oriental
Languages and Literatures

Latin on Media Show

Participation in Office of University Computing's Educational Technology Summer Workshop allowed me to experiment with some ideas about the presentation of Late Antique and Medieval Latin texts. The typical pedagogy, centuries old, for the study of Latin texts beyond the elementary level involves the students "working up" in advance an assigned text which is then reviewed in detail in class. They then take turns translating in class, a format which provides a common experience of the text and an opportunity for verification/correction of students' understandings through the instructor's commentary and elucidation of the text.

Contemporary English is only vestigially inflected, and the fundamental problem of students in reading Latin is their insensitivity to the visual cues to differentiation and meaning in that highly inflected language. In short, they see but they do not observe. I had experimented earlier with the use of opaque and overhead projectors to present Latin texts to classes. Visual presentation increases ease of reference to the text (pointing, as opposed to giving verbal cues for the location of a phrase, word, or syllable), and makes the encounter with the text in class more of a common visual experience (as opposed to solitary staring into solitary books with information shared only in the auditory medium). This sort of display also allows alternative visual presentations of the text. E.g., instead of block paragraphs, one can display an unpunctuated phrase by phrase presentation (called in Latin per cola et commata) to aid in the mental process that psychologists of reading call "chunking"; presenting verse as prose, without the usual colometry challenges trite assumptions about the character of poetry, etc.

Figure 1. MediaShow

MediaShow, a HyperCard-based tool developed at Notre Dame, allows scrolled presentation of extensive texts loaded as text files. These files were both typed up as Microsoft Word files or loaded via optical scanner and stored after correction as Microsoft Word files. An added "blackboard" button brings up a blank screen onto which sections of text can be copied or typed, with rearrangement, insertions, etc., for discussion with the visual aid of the tool kit. A bonus to my original scheme was the option of displaying images of earlier ways of presenting/transmitting the text, i.e., photographs of text and illustration from late antique and medieval manuscripts and early printed books.

I feel that this method of presenting texts offers great promise. One semester's experience with it suggests the following: 1) More class time should be devoted to using this method of visual presentation at the first stages of students' encounter with the texts, i.e., to aid in their examination of the text by showing them what to see and how to see it. 2) Hardware in DeBartolo Hall for presenting images must be improved; the images of manuscript pages lose a lot due to the current projection system, however good the initial photography. 3) We need to find ways to make the resources of DeBartolo available in a way appropriate to small class-seminar teaching, i.e., to make full use of computer and screen while retaining the intimacy of the small interactive group.

Ursula Williams
Director
Language Resource Center

Using Media in Foreign Language Instruction

One way to learn French would be simply to move to
France. This is called "total immersion," and is very effective.
The structure of the language would be internalized as a by-
product of the need to speak enough of it to survive.

Initially, "survival French" might be rough and spotty; one
has to assume a degree of intellectual curiosity that would
spur a desire to move to a higher level. It is easy to see that
such phrases as, "Can you tell me where the bathrooms are?"
might be learned very quickly, while others, like, "The young
boy gives the brown spotted dog a big red ball," might never
be uttered at all. Total immersion language learning is rooted
in reality. Given the demands of our lives, it would be
impractical, even though undeniably useful, to move to
France for a few years just to learn the language. But there
would be advantages: learning quickly; learning authentic
rhythm and pronunciation; learning body language, that
system of gestures and postures unique to every language;
gaining at the same time language ability and cultural
fluency, the sense of what makes life in France different from
life in the United States. (And there's that wonderful bread.)
There is a practical alternative. It sounds trite, but it's true:
we can bring France (except the bread) into the classroom.
We can do it with media.

One way to bring a variety of material into the classroom has always been audio-visual media. (Another is *realia*. Language teachers are well-known for bringing foreign newspapers, subway tickets, restaurant menus and the like to class.) The need to augment textbook and classroom instruction with authentic language input has been felt almost since the beginning. The development of the language lab in the early sixties was not only a reaction to the high-tech and foreign language education scare provoked by the launch of Sputnik by the Soviet Union a few years earlier. It may also have been the first time a consumer item—the tape recorder—was adapted for education. The tape recorder was a compact, relatively inexpensive means of bringing the voices of native speakers into the classroom. One unfortunate result was the development of exercises that are now often called "drill 'n kill." But the *multiple media* concept in foreign language education has been there all along, and the audio tape is still one component of that concept, as evidenced at Notre Dame by its continuing presence in the Language Resource Center in O'Shaughnessy Hall. Audio tape is still a cheap, easy, portable way for students to practice by recording their own voices.

The next consumer item to make its way into the classroom was the video tape recorder (VCR). The advantage of providing current, portable, lifelike moving pictures for class compensated for the bulk, noise and capricious behavior of the early VCR. The machinery has improved, but the problem with video tape continues to be the difficulty of moving around between discrete segments. For the most part video tape is designed to be viewed in a linear fashion; that is, in a straight pass from beginning to end. Rewinding and fast-forwarding take time, are imprecise, and shorten the life of the tape. The introduction of the CAV (constant angular velocity) video disc, or laser disc, which can contain the same linear half-hour of video, also made it possible to rethink the way video can be used. Each frame (54,000 of them on one side) of a CAV video disc has an identifying mark that enables the video disc player or a computer to locate and display it. The 54,000 frames can be shown singly, as still frames, in an endless number of unique sequential possibilities, (not truly endless; actually the number is: 230,843,697,339,241,380,472,092,742,683,027,581,083,278,564,571,807,941,132,288,000,000,000,000) or as a half hour of full motion video with two soundtrack possibilities, or as a random assortment of video clips. Anyone who has ever been asked to show slide #27 again when they happen to be showing slide #42 can appreciate the utility of instant random access. In the time it takes to enter a few numbers into a remote control or click a mouse on a computer, the next image appears. The CD-ROM has the same functionality and the advantage of being completely digital in format. It can hold 72 minutes of full-motion video in a much smaller package, and will probably replace the video disc.

There is no doubt that the addition of media adds dimension to language study. But the concept of media in the foreign language classroom was revolutionized in 1987 with the introduction of the first video-based foreign language course. Developed at Yale University by Pierre Capretz, the program, called *French in Action* was adopted at Notre Dame in 1989. It consists of 52 lessons, each of which builds around a video segment. Text-based materials support the course, but each lesson is introduced entirely on video. A video-based course changes language instruction by placing the emphasis on communication, thus shifting the focus to *acquisition*.

Media offer input of tremendous quantity and variety, and address variety in learning styles. Some learning styles favor text; others, perhaps more of them now that a generation has grown up in a decidedly image-oriented environment, fare better when images are part of the process. If the images are integrated into the course and don't merely exist as a temporary diversion from text-based learning, they serve to enhance the acquisition of knowledge in a dramatic way.

Here's what can be learned in the very first *French in Action* lesson: how French people dress; what streets and houses and cars in France look like; that French people seem to stand quite a bit closer together when they converse; that French people seem to kiss both cheeks or shake hands on greeting and taking leave of one another; that French people's mouths look different from American people's mouths when they speak because they seem to use their lips much more to form "rounder" o's and u's; and that "Je vais" seems to mean "I am going." This last point is so clearly made by the images in the first lesson that it is impossible to miss. It seems redundant to talk about it. Nonetheless one does talk about it in class, because when second language acquisition and learning take place at this late stage of life, the process can be hastened by adding the study of grammar and structure to large doses of authentic input. There is a limit. The amount of language acquired from understanding authentic input levels off at a certain point. After that, reading adds the necessary dimension. A very high level of linguistic competency is the ability to read the literature of the land, to discover the uniqueness of experience that is written there, leading to a closer understanding of what it means to be French, and more about what it means to be American.

French In Action is an example of a bold jump into a method in which images are the springboard for learning. The video disc has made it possible to manipulate still or moving pictures in a user-determined way, as opposed to the way they were originally placed. The Media-On-Call system in DeBartolo Hall is an extension of this kind of non-linear thinking. It permits user-determined sequences of media to be used in language instruction. The trend is clearly toward more types of media. Language instructors at Notre Dame who a few years ago used the occasional audio tape to bring additional authentic input to class now use tapes, CD's, video tapes and video discs. All of these are available for outside-of-class learning as well. The "lab" now also includes computers, which add foreign language word processing, drills with immediate feedback, international e-mail, live international "chat" and usenet news, and interactive programs in which the learner, who has to understand a variety of input to move forward, determines the outcome of events. All of these together come very close to providing total immersion, albeit in smaller doses, but with many of the advantages, and, unfortunately, without the bread.

Jump Start Grant Awards
1992-1994

Tom Frecka
Department of Accountancy

Tammy Mittelstaedt
Department of Accountancy

Michael Morris
Department of Accountancy

Juan Rivera
Department of Accountancy

Ramachandran Ramanan
Department of Accountancy

Norlin Rueschhoff
Department of Accountancy

Tom Schlereth
Department of American Studies

Martin Murphy
Department of Anthropology

Norman Crowe
Department of Architecture

Chuck Rosenberg
Department of Art

John Adams
Department of Biological Sciences

Harald Esch
Department of Biological Sciences

Douglas McAbee
Department of Biological Sciences

Marjie Yarger
Computer Applications Program

Kathy Sexton
Center for Pastoral Liturgy

Anne Montgomery
English as a Foreign Language Program

Eduardo Wolf
Department of Chemical Engineering

Paul Helquist
Department of Chemistry

Dennis Jacobs
Department of Chemistry

Jim Johnson
Department of Chemistry

James Keller
Department of Chemistry

Marv Miller
Department of Chemistry

Michael Brownstein
Department of Classical/Oriental Language and Literature

George Minamiki
Department of Classical/Oriental Language and Literature

Dan Sheerin
Department of Classical/Oriental Language and Literature

Bruce Auerbach
Department of Communication and Theatre

Richard Donnelly
Department of Communication and Theatre

Kevin Dreyer
Department of Communication and Theatre

Jay Brockman
Department of Computer Science & Engineering

Andrew Lumsdaine
Department of Computer Science & Engineering

Phil Mirowski
Department of Economics

Erskine Peters
Department of English

Margo Axsom
Department of English and American Literature

James Dougherty
Department of English and American Literature

Sandra Hayes
Department of English and American Literature

Lew Soens
Department of English and American Literature

John Halloran
Department of Finance

Barry Keating
Department of Finance

Robert Baker
Freshman Writing Program

Peggy DeBoer
Freshman Writing Program

Ed Klein
Freshman Writing Program

Irene Leahy
Freshman Writing Program

Jean Anne Strebinger
Freshman Writing Program

Uma Balakrishnan
Department of Government

Bob Johansen
Department of Government

Sharon O'Brien
Department of Government

Thomas Kselman
Department of History

Patti Ogden
Law Library

John Weber
Department of Marketing

A. Alexandrou Himonas
Department of Mathematics

Rod Lekey
Naval Science

David Burrell
Department of Philosophy

Thomas Morris
Department of Philosophy

Sun-Joo Shin
Department of Philosophy

Lyn Spillman
Department of Sociology

Rich Williams
Department of Sociology

Bob Krieg
Department of Theology

Thomas O'Meara
Department of Theology

Anne McGuire
Department of Theology

Gerald Schlabach
Department of Theology

Kern Trembath
Department of Theology